HOW TO UNDERSTAND

ACCOUNTS

ouse

How to Understand Accounts
by David Rouse

1st edition 2007
   Reprinted 2008

Lawpack Publishing Limited
76–89 Alscot Road
London SE1 3AW

www.lawpack.co.uk

ISBN: 978-1-905261-58-1

Exclusion of Liability and Disclaimer

Contents

To the memory of my beloved wife, Julia, and for my son, Thomas.

About the author

David Rouse is a chartered accountant with many years' experience advising businesses and other organisations on accountancy and related financial matters. He has worked for major national and international accountancy firms and he has also run his own small practice. He now provides technical consultancy services and writes in-house manuals for other accountants in practice.

Introduction

What are accounts?

Before trying to understand accounts, the term needs to be explained. In this context, the accounts of a business or other organisation are financial statements showing:

- what has happened for a given period in the past; and
- the position at the end of that period.

The statement showing what has happened in the past is usually called the Profit and Loss Account (see Chapter 1). A club, or an organisation that is not operating a business, may call the statement an Income and Expenditure Account. A Profit and Loss Account and an Income and Expenditure Account show the sales and other income of the organisation from which the expenses are deducted. When the income is in excess of the expenses the result is called 'a profit' in a Profit and Loss Account, or a 'surplus' in an Income and Expenditure Account. When the expenses are greater than the income the result is called a 'loss' in a Profit and Loss Account, or a 'deficit' in an Income and Expenditure Account.

The statement showing the position at the end of the period is called the Balance Sheet (see Chapter 2). This shows what is owned by the organisation, the money owing to and by the organisation, and the money invested in the organisation by its proprietors or members.

In addition to the Profit and Loss Account and Balance Sheet there will usually be notes to explain some of the figures in more detail. In some cases there may also be a Cash Flow Statement (see Chapter 3), which shows where the cash has come from and where it has gone.

A full set of accounts consisting of a Profit and Loss Account, Balance Sheet, Notes to the Accounts (see Chapter 4) and, in some cases, a Cash Flow Statement, may be referred to as 'financial statements'. Notes to the Accounts provide further details about figures shown in the Profit and Loss Account, Balance Sheet and Cash Flow Statement, as well as additional information to help the reader understand the accounts.

Other chapters in this book explain each part of the accounts in more detail and they take a critical look at example accounts so that you can obtain a better understanding.

Who needs to understand accounts?

Accounts are prepared by accountants, but there are many more people who can benefit from an understanding of them, including anyone:

- owning and running a business as a sole trader or partner;
- working in a company as a director;
- employed in the management of a business in any capacity;
- owning shares in a company;
- interested in buying a business;
- interested in selling a business;
- involved in the management of a club, charity or other organisation;
- employed in a job that involves looking at accounts;
- investing in the stock market;
- wishing to improve their knowledge of accounts.

For some people, an understanding of accounts is essential. In most cases a trained accountant will actually prepare the accounts of a business, but the proprietors or directors have the responsibility for approving those accounts. This does not mean that they are expected to have the knowledge needed to prepare the accounts, but they are expected to understand and approve the figures included in those accounts.

Anyone who is self-employed has full responsibility for the figures entered on their tax returns, no matter who actually prepares the accounts. Company directors are assumed to be aware of the financial position of their companies, even though they may employ someone else to prepare the accounts. A director who continues trading when he knows, or ought to have known, that the company cannot pay its debts may be required to pay compensation and could be barred from being a director in the future.

Who needs accounts?

Accounts are used to manage and explain the operation of a business or other organisation and so are important for the managers and owners or anyone involved in the running of the organisation. In addition, accounts are often required for legal or other reasons:

HM Revenue & Customs

Accounts are required to show the profits on which tax is paid or the losses on which tax relief can be claimed.

Accounts are also required for businesses registered for VAT to assist HM Revenue & Customs in agreeing VAT liabilities.

Companies House

Limited companies must file accounts at Companies House annually.

Unlimited companies only need to file accounts if the company is a subsidiary or a parent of a limited company. However, unlimited companies are extremely rare and all subsequent references in this book to companies relate to limited companies.

Banks and other lenders

Banks and other lenders usually require accounts in support of applications for loans.

Charities

There are legal requirements for charities to prepare accounts and, except for very small charities, accounts must be filed with the Charity Commission. Its website is www.charity-commission.gov.uk.

Industrial and provident societies

There are legal requirements for organisations registered under the Industrial and Provident Societies Acts to prepare and file accounts. Organisations, such as sports clubs and community associations, may register under the Industrial and Provident Societies Acts instead of registering as companies under the Companies Acts. Registration gives the benefit of limited liability in the same way as a limited company and the accounting requirements are similar to those for companies. Registration is with the Financial Services Authority (FSA) and annual accounts are filed with the FSA. Its website is www.fsa.gov.uk.

Others

Accounts may also be required by trade and other organisations, and for the purpose of obtaining grants, etc. Bodies providing grants include the government, the European Union and local authorities. Grants may be available for a variety of purposes, including research and development, training and energy efficiency. Useful information is available on www.businesslink.gov.uk.

Understanding accounts

The guidance in this book assumes that the reader does not have any previous accountancy knowledge. It is a guide to understanding, rather than preparing, accounts. The Appendices include examples of different types of accounts, as well as checklists for reviewing accounts, troubleshooting and stocktaking. In addition, Appendix K explains the treatment of Value Added Tax (VAT) in the accounts.

CHAPTER 1

The Trading and Profit and Loss Account

Overview

The Trading and Profit and Loss Account is a summary of the trading carried on by a business during a given period and shows the profit or loss of the business after taking into account expenses.

The make up of the Trading and Profit and Loss Account is normally as follows:

		£
A	Sales	*
B	Cost of sales	*
C	Gross profit (A – B)	*
D	Expenses	*
E	Net profit or loss (C – D)	*

The Trading and Profit and Loss Account is divided into two parts. The Trading Account ends at the gross profit and the Profit and Loss Account covers the rest of the statement. Sometimes the whole statement, from sales to net profit or loss, is simply referred to as the Profit and Loss Account.

Examples of Profit and Loss Accounts are shown in Appendices A.1, B.1, C.2, C5 and D. These are discussed later in this chapter.

Sales

Where invoices are always issued to customers for sales, the figure shown in the accounts for sales is the total of all the sales invoices issued in the period (excluding VAT) with the following deductions:

- Credit notes issued against sales made before the end of the period (excluding VAT).

- Trade discounts allowed to customers (see below).

All sales made in the period are included, whether or not the customer has paid by the end of the period.

VAT charged to customers is not included with the sales figure, as this has to be paid over to HM Revenue & Customs (HMRC).

Where all sales are paid for immediately, as in a retail business where credit is not given, the sales figure will be the same as the total cash received from customers, excluding VAT.

Sales only include goods in which the business normally trades. They do not include sales of fixed assets used in the business (e.g. buildings, plant and machinery, motor vehicles, etc. – see Chapter 2).

Where the business involves the provision of a service, the term 'sales' may not be appropriate. In this case the heading could be 'fees' or 'work done'. The term 'turnover' is sometimes used to cover all types of sales and services.

Where a business has several different types of sales, the total for each type may be shown separately.

Trade discounts are allowances made to customers for various reasons. They could be based on quantities sold, type of product, status of customer, etc. and they are usually deducted on the invoice to arrive at the net sales figure. Trade discounts do not normally depend on the date that payment is made.

Cash discounts are allowances that depend on payment being made by the customer, either immediately or within a specific period. Cash discounts are not usually deducted from the sales figure but are shown as a separate item of expense in the Profit and Loss Account.

Goods for own use

If the proprietor takes goods out of the business and pays for them as a customer, the amount paid will be included in the sales figure. If the proprietor does not pay for the goods, the selling price is shown as income under the heading 'goods for own use', or 'personal consumption', so that the treatment is effectively as if it were a sale. If the goods are only partly paid for and it is not intended to pay the balance, the amount paid would be included in the sales figure and the unpaid part under the heading 'goods for own use'. The amount included in goods for own use is also included in drawings as the goods have been taken out of the business by the proprietor without his paying for them.

Goods for own use and drawings are explained further in Chapter 2. An example is shown in Appendices B.1 and B.3. Partner A has this year taken goods for his own use from the partnership amounting to £2,000 and this is shown in Appendix B.1 as income in the Profit and Loss Account and as drawings in note 5 to the accounts in Appendix B.3.

Cost of sales

Cost of sales is the direct cost to the business of all the items included in the sales figure. In a simple business buying and selling goods, the cost of sales is the amount that the business paid to its suppliers for the goods that have been sold. Where the business is registered for VAT, the cost of sales does not include VAT as this is reclaimed from HMRC. Cost of sales for a business not registered for VAT will include VAT, as this is part of the cost to the business and it cannot be recovered from HMRC. A business must register for VAT when the turnover is above a specified level. The current level can be found on HMRC's website at www.hmrc.gov.uk.

In a manufacturing business there will be a number of items making up the cost of sales. These will include the cost of raw materials and parts used in the manufacture, the wages for the employees directly involved in the manufacture, the costs (such as electricity) to operate machinery used in the manufacture and any other direct costs involved in bringing the product into a condition to be sold.

In a business providing a service, the direct cost of providing that service will normally be the salary costs of the employees directly involved in earning the fees.

Although it may be possible in some businesses to keep a record showing the cost of each individual item sold, the cost of sales is more often arrived at by putting together total figures as follows:

		£
A	Opening stock and work-in-progress	*
B	Purchases and other direct costs	*
C	(A + B)	*
D	Closing stock and work-in-progress	*
E	Cost of sales (C − D)	*

Opening and closing stock and work-in-progress are valued at the cost to the business, excluding VAT if the business is registered for VAT but including VAT if the business is not registered for VAT.

For example, if a product which costs the business £60 is sold for £100 and ten items are sold in the period for a total of £1,000, the total cost of sales is 10 x £60 = £600. If there were four items in stock at the beginning of the period, eight items bought during the period and two items in stock at the end of the period, the figures would be as follows:

		£
A	Opening stock (4 x £60)	240
B	Purchases (8 x £60)	480
C	(A + B)	720
D	Closing stock (2 x £60)	120
E	Cost of sales (C − D)	600

Gross profit

Gross profit is the amount left after deducting the cost of sales from the sales figure. Using the figures from the above example, the sales total is £1,000 and the cost of sales is £600, giving a gross profit of £400.

The gross profit percentage is an important figure to look at. This is the gross profit expressed as a percentage of sales. In the example above, the gross profit of £400 gives a gross profit percentage of 40 per cent, being £400 expressed as a percentage of £1,000 (see also Chapter 5).

Expenses

General

The expenses listed after the gross profit are not directly linked to the level of production or sales. They are for the benefit of the business as a whole. These expenses are usually referred to as 'overheads' or 'indirect expenses'. They cover selling, distribution, administration and all other costs that are not included in the cost of sales.

Some expenses can be described as 'fixed expenses'. Examples are rent and rates, which are unchanged whether sales increase or decrease.

Overheads that change, to some extent according to the level of business, are called 'variable' or 'semi-variable expenses'. Telephone charges may be semi-variable. The rental part of the charge is fixed, while the cost of calls varies according to the extent to which the telephone is used.

Expenses are included in the Profit and Loss Account in the period in which they are incurred, even though payment may not be made until after the end of the period. In some cases the business may not even receive an invoice until some time after the end of the period. For example:

- Your accountant's fees for preparing the accounts may not be invoiced to the business until the work has been completed after the end of the year. However, the agreed fee, or an estimate, is included as an expense in the accounts being prepared. This does not affect the date that the invoice is actually sent or the date of payment.

- Bills for electricity will be issued periodically, perhaps quarterly. For example, if the financial year end is 30 September, the last bill issued before 30 September may have covered electricity used to the end of July. The next bill would cover the three months to the end of October. Unless an adjustment is made, the Profit and Loss Account for the year ended 30 September will not include a charge for the electricity used in the months of August and September as the bill will not be issued until after the end of September. An estimate to cover those two months is therefore included in the accounts and is called an 'accrual'.

Some expenses are paid in advance. For example, an annual insurance premium paid on 1 July covers the business for the next 12 months ending on 30 June in the following year. If the financial year end is 30 September, only three months of the premium relates to the current year ended 30 September. An adjustment is made to carry forward into the next financial year that part of the premium covering the nine months to the following 30 June. The amount carried forward is called a 'prepayment'. A similar adjustment will have been made in the accounts ended 30 September in the previous year in respect of the premium paid on 1 July in the previous year. The accounts for the year ended 30 September in the current year (year 2) therefore include an insurance charge covering the full 12 months made up as follows:

- Nine months to 30 June in year 2 is the prepayment brought forward from the previous year (year 1), being three-quarters of the premium paid on 1 July in year 1.

- Three months to 30 September in year 2 is part of the premium paid on 1 July in year 2. The balance of the premium paid on 1 July in year 2, representing nine months to 30 June in year 3, is carried forward and charged in the accounts for the year ending 30 September in year 3.

Expenses charged in the Profit and Loss Account do not include reclaimable VAT. If the business is not VAT registered, VAT should be included with the expense item to which it relates.

Accruals and prepayments are also discussed in Chapter 2.

Expense headings

The expense headings can be varied to suit each individual business.
expenses may be listed in a single column (e.g. as in the sole trader's Profit
and Loss Account shown in Appendix A.1) or grouped under appropriate
headings with totals for each group of expenses (e.g. as in the partnership
Profit and Loss Account shown in Appendix B.1). The following are
examples of expense groups that are often used showing some of the types
of expenses that would be included under each heading:

Selling

- Salespersons' salaries
- Advertising
- Travel and motor expenses
- Entertaining

Establishment (or premises)

- Rent
- Rates
- Light and heat
- Property insurance
- Property repairs

Administration

- Office salaries
- Telephone
- Postage
- Printing and stationery
- Accountancy
- Legal and professional charges
- Bad debts

- Bank interest
- Hire purchase interest
- Loan interest

Revenue and capital expenditure

A distinction must be made between capital and revenue expenditure. Capital expenditure belongs on the Balance Sheet, while revenue expenditure is included in the Profit and Loss Account as a deduction from profits. Money spent on fixed assets (see Chapter 2) is capital expenditure and sometimes the distinction is clear. For example:

- The cost of a new car is capital expenditure.
- The cost of petrol to run the car is revenue expenditure.

Sometimes the distinction is less certain. For example:

- Alterations or improvements to a building are normally capital expenditure.
- Restoring a building to its original condition is normally revenue expenditure.

The distinction between capital and revenue expenditure is important not just for the presentation of the accounts but also for tax reasons. Revenue expenditure may be allowed as a deduction from profits for tax purposes, whereas there may be no tax relief for capital expenditure or only part of the expenditure may be allowed against tax each year by way of capital allowances.

Depreciation is not allowed as a deduction from profits for tax purposes as any business is free to set whatever level of depreciation it considers appropriate. However, allowances can be claimed on the cost of fixed assets at various rates specified by tax law, according to the type of fixed asset. These are known as 'capital allowances'. Allowances may be claimed on the initial cost and then annually, as long as the fixed asset is in use by the business.

In order to arrive at the taxable profits, it is necessary to add back to the net profit shown in the accounts any depreciation that has been deducted in arriving at that net profit (and also add back any other expenses not allowable for tax purposes) and then deduct the capital allowances claimed.

The line showing additions to fixtures and fittings of £800 in note 1 to the accounts in Appendix A.3 is an example of capital expenditure incurred during the year. The expenses shown in the Profit and Loss Account in Appendix A.1 are all revenue expenditure.

Loan and hire purchase repayments

Loan and hire purchase repayments will usually consist of both interest and capital. The interest part of the repayment is revenue expenditure to be shown in the Profit and Loss Account while the capital part, reducing the original amount borrowed, is deducted from the balance of the loan shown on the Balance Sheet (see Chapter 2).

Salaries

Gross salaries (i.e. before deducting PAYE and employees' National Insurance, etc.) are charged in the Profit and Loss Account together with the employer's National Insurance. Sometimes the employer's National Insurance is shown separately.

Money taken out of the business by the proprietor or partners is not charged as an expense in the Profit and Loss Account. It is dealt with as drawings and charged to the proprietor's or partners' current accounts shown in the Balance Sheet (see Chapter 2).

Where the business is a company, salaries paid to directors are normally dealt with as expenses in the Profit and Loss Account. For most purposes company directors are treated as employees of the company, whereas a sole trader or partner is the owner, or part owner, of the business. Shareholders are the owners of a company and, although shareholders are often also directors, a distinction is made between money paid to a person as a director (normally a 'salary') and as a shareholder (normally a 'dividend'). Dividends paid to shareholders are not charged as expenses in the Profit and Loss Account before arriving at the net profit. Dividends are a distribution of net profit to the owners of the company.

Company accounts are dealt with more fully in Chapter 4.

Insurance

Only business insurance is included. Other types of insurance, such as the proprietor's personal life insurance when the beneficiaries are the proprietor's family rather than the business, are usually charged to drawings (see Chapter 2).

Personal pension contributions paid for a sole trader or partner are dealt with as drawings. Tax relief may be available to the sole trader or partner personally. Company pension contributions paid for a company director are normally charged as expenses in the Profit and Loss Account. Tax relief is normally available to the company and not the director personally. A great deal of useful information on tax matters, including tax relief, can be obtained from HMRC's website at www.hmrc.gov.uk.

Bad debts

All sales invoiced to customers are included in the sales figure (unless they are cancelled by credit notes), even if the customer never pays. If it becomes necessary to write off an amount owing by a customer, the amount written off is shown as a 'bad debt'. Normally a bad debt will only be completely written off in the books when it has been established beyond any doubt that payment will never be received (e.g. if the customer is bankrupt and no funds are available to pay creditors). Sometimes a debt is considered doubtful without giving up all hope of recovery. Doubtful debts are included with bad debts written off in the Profit and Loss Account. The heading 'bad debts' may sometimes be changed to 'bad and doubtful debts' to make this clear. If a bad or doubtful debt is subsequently recovered in a future year, the amount recovered is either set off against any other bad debts charged in the Profit and Loss Account or shown separately as an addition to profit under the heading 'bad debts recovered'.

Depreciation

Fixed assets, such as fixtures and fittings and motor vehicles, are usually of benefit to a business for a number of years. Depreciation aims to write down the cost of fixed assets over their expected useful lives so that a fair proportion of the cost is allocated to each accounting period expected to benefit from their use.

The two usual ways of calculating depreciation are straight line and reducing balance.

Straight line

Depreciation is calculated on the cost of the asset so that the same amount of depreciation is charged each year. For example:

Cost of asset – £4,000

Depreciation – 25% straight line

Depreciation charge is £1,000 each year for four years

At the end of the fourth year the value of the asset in the books is NIL

		£	£
Cost of asset			4,000
Depreciation	- Year 1	1,000	
	- Year 2	1,000	
	- Year 3	1,000	
	- Year 4	1,000	
			4,000
Book value at end of year 4			NIL

Reducing balance

In the first year depreciation is calculated on the cost of the asset and in future years on the written down book value. The written down book value is the figure remaining after deducting all the depreciation to date from the original cost. For example:

Cost of asset – £4,000

Depreciation – 25% reducing balance

Depreciation - Year 1 – 25% of £4,000   = £1,000

         - Year 2 – 25% of £3,000 (£4,000 – £1,000) = £750

         - Year 3 – 25% of £2,250 (£3,000 – £750)   = £563

         - Year 4 – 25% of £1,687 (£2,250 – £563)   = £422

At the end of the fourth year the value of the asset in the books is £1,265 as shown below:

		£	£
Cost of asset			4,000
Depreciation	- Year 1	1,000	
	- Year 2	750	
	- Year 3	563	
	- Year 4	422	
			2,735
Book value at end of year 4			1,265

Profit/loss on sale of fixed assets

When a fixed asset is sold or scrapped, the difference between the sale proceeds and the net book value at the time of the sale is either a profit on sale (where the sale proceeds are more than the net book value) or a loss on sale (where the sale proceeds are less than the net book value).

Use of home

Where a business pays rent for a property used in the business the cost of the rent is charged as an expense in the Profit and Loss Account. If the proprietor uses part of his home in the business, perhaps as an office, which may be either a room set aside exclusively for the business or a room used partly for business and partly for domestic purposes, a charge can be included in the Profit and Loss Account to cover the cost of light and heat, etc. for the time that the room is used for business. The proprietor is given credit in the proprietor's current account for the amount included as use of home and it is treated in a similar way to cash introduced into the business and any other business expenses paid privately. This is explained further in Chapter 2.

Private proportions

Certain expenses may be partly in respect of the business and partly for private purposes. For example, a car used in the business will almost certainly be used for private purposes as well. A log should be kept of all business mileage to work out how to allocate the cost of motor expenses (petrol, repairs, etc.) between business and private use. If the total annual mileage is 10,000 miles and 6,000 of these are for business purposes, motor expenses are allocated 60 per cent as business (an expense in the Profit and Loss Account) and 40 per cent as private (drawings).

Telephone is another expense that may sometimes have a private proportion and a record should be kept of all calls to be allocated between business and private use.

Sometimes the full cost of motor expenses and telephone, etc. is charged in the Profit and Loss Account and an adjustment is made in the tax computation instead of charging the private proportions to drawings. When a company director or other employee uses a car owned by the business for private purposes then the full car expenses, being both business and private, may be charged as an expense in the Profit and Loss Account and the director or employee is taxed personally on the private element as if it were additional salary. Other personal expenses paid by the business and included as expenses in the Profit and Loss Account are dealt with in a similar way. Such expenses paid by the business for the benefit of a director or employee are known as 'benefits in kind'.

Net profit/loss

All the expenses are deducted from gross profit to arrive at the net profit. There is a net loss if the total expenses are more than the gross profit. If the business is a sole trader (or partnership), the net profit or loss is transferred to the proprietor's current account. In a limited company the profit is available for distribution to shareholders, normally by way of dividends, and the balance is transferred to the company's reserves (see Chapter 4).

Examples of Trading and Profit and Loss Accounts

A sole trader (Appendix A.1)

In this year the sales are £120,000. The cost of these sales to the business is £90,000. Cost of sales is deducted from sales to give a gross profit of £30,000. The expenses, which include adjustments for accruals and prepayments, amount to £34,640 and this figure is deducted from the gross profit. As the expenses are more than the gross profit there is a net loss of £4,640. There is further discussion on this Trading and Profit and Loss Account in Chapter 5 where the accounts for a sole trader are used in a case study.

A partnership (Appendix B.1)

This year the sales are £409,337. One of the partners has taken goods for his own use amounting to £2,000 from the business and this is added to give a sub-total of £411,337. The cost of sales of £305,810 is deducted and the result is a gross profit of £105,527. Opening and closing stock has not been shown as two separate figures in the cost of sales, as was the case in the Trading and Profit and Loss Account for a sole trader. The partnership closing stock was £2,550 less than the opening stock and is shown on one line as a stock decrease. This is simply an alternative way of showing the stock figures and is a matter of personal choice. There is some other income amounting to £2,130, which is added to the gross profit to give a profit before expenses of £107,657. Expenses have been grouped into four different headings, 'establishment', 'selling and distribution', 'administration' and 'financial', the details of each group being shown on the second page of Appendix B.1. The total of expenses is £60,515 and this figure is deducted from the gross profit and other income to give a net profit of £47,142. Sometimes 'other income' is not shown on the Profit and Loss Account until after the expenses so that the reader can see the profit before other income is added. The net profit is allocated to the two partners by giving partner A a salary of £10,000 with the balance divided equally. There was no salary last year. The allocation of profit between partners can be in whatever proportions the partners agree. There would usually be a formal partnership agreement drawn up as a legal document so that it is clear how profits are to be allocated.

A small company (Appendix C.5)

The business involves the sale and repairs of office machinery and sales have been analysed between the two activities. The sales total is £811,337 from which the cost of sales figure of £583,229 is deducted to give a gross profit of £228,108. The wages of £52,546 included in the cost of sales figure relate to the employees who carried out the repairs to customers' machinery, which have earned £107,925. If the information is available to analyse stock and purchases between different activities, in this case between office machinery repairs and sales, separate trading accounts may be prepared showing the gross profit for each activity. Bank interest received of £230 is added to the gross profit (to make £228,338) and expenses totalling £169,919 are deducted to give a net profit of £58,419. Expenses have been analysed into four groups with the details shown on the second page of Appendix C.5.

There are two examples of the statutory formats of the Profit and Loss Account for a small company in Appendices C.2 and D and these are explained in Chapter 4.

Income and Expenditure Account

In some organisations it may not be appropriate to refer to a profit or loss.

For example, a club or charity will have income and expenditure, but the organisation is not run to make a profit in the same way that a business operates to make a profit. Such organisations will prepare accounts in a similar way to those prepared by a business, but the summary of income and expenditure may be called an Income and Expenditure Account instead of a Profit and Loss Account. An excess of income over expenditure is called a 'surplus', instead of 'profit', and an excess of expenditure over income is called a 'deficit', instead of a 'loss'.

There are special rules for the way that larger charities prepare their accounts and the Income and Expenditure Account is called the Statement of Financial Activities. Income is referred to as 'incoming resources' and expenditure is referred to as 'resources expended'. The difference between incoming resources and resources expended is referred to as 'net incoming (or outgoing) resources'.

Whatever they may be called, an Income and Expenditure Account or Statement of Financial Activities are both variations of a Profit and Loss Account.

Receipts and Payments Account

It should be understood that a Receipts and Payments Account is not a variation of a Profit and Loss Account; it is something quite different. A Profit and Loss Account takes into account accruals and prepayments and it does not include capital items, such as fixed assets, which appear on the Balance Sheet. A Receipts and Payments Account, however, does not take into account accruals and prepayments and it includes capital items.

As the name suggests, the Receipts and Payments Account is a summary of all money received from whatever source and all money paid for whatever purpose during the period. It will therefore not include any depreciation, as this is not money paid out, but it will include money received for the sale of fixed assets and money paid for the purchase of fixed assets. The Receipts and Payments Account also shows the money held at the beginning of the period and the money held at the end of the period, whether in cash or in a bank account. It does not show a profit or loss.

It may be prepared in either horizontal form or vertical form and examples of each are shown in Appendices G.1 and G.2. The vertical form clearly shows the movement in cash for the period and this figure should not be confused with profit or loss. The Receipts and Payments Account is, in effect, a type of Cash Flow Statement, which is discussed in Chapter 3. It is a much simpler document than the Profit and Loss Account and Balance Sheet and is often prepared by small clubs and charities as an alternative to a full set of accounts.

CHAPTER 2

The Balance Sheet

Overview

The Balance Sheet shows the state of the business, or other organisation, at one particular point in time, i.e. the close of business on the date to which the accounts are prepared. There are two equal sides to a Balance Sheet. At one time it was usual to show one side on the left and the other on the right but now the two sides are usually shown on a single page, one side on top of the other. On occasions, larger Balance Sheets are shown on two separate pages with one side on each page.

The side usually shown first is a list of the assets and liabilities. The total of this side, the net assets, is arrived at by deducting the total liabilities from the total assets. The other side shows the funds provided to finance the net assets. These funds consist mainly of long-term capital that has been put into the business and profits that have been left in the business.

The basic layout of the Balance Sheet is as follows:

		£	£
A	Fixed assets		*
B	Current assets	*	
C	Current liabilities	*	
D	Net current assets (or liabilities) (B – C)		*

E	(A + D)	*
F	Liabilities due after more than one year	*
G	Total assets less liabilities (E – F)	*
	Financed by:	
H	Capital	*
I	Undrawn profits	*
J	Total proprietor's funds (H + I)	*

G is equal to J

When the business is a sole trader (or partnership), the capital is the money put into the business by the proprietor and is shown on the Balance Sheet as the capital account. There could also be long-term loans put into the business by someone other than the proprietor. The undrawn profits left in the business are represented by the balance on the proprietor's current account, being the amount left after deducting drawings from profits. Sometimes the capital and current accounts are combined and the single account is called simply the 'capital account'.

Capital and current accounts are illustrated in Appendix B.3, notes 4 and 5 to the accounts. Note 4 shows that a total of £10,000 long-term capital had been put into the business by the partners in previous years and a further £2,500 was paid in by partner A this year, giving a total of £12,500 to be left in the business for the forseeable future. Note 5 shows that the partners had left a total of £14,465 in the business from accumulated net profits earned in previous years. A profit of £47,142 has been earned this year, but the partners have only taken out a total of £16,929 in drawings and goods for own use this year, leaving £45,088 carried forward into next year. This is not treated as long-term capital, although the partners may leave it in the business as long as they wish.

Although some businesses may combine the capital and current accounts and call the single account a 'capital account', this terminology can be confusing as the balance on the account is not all long-term capital and some of it may be drawn out in the near future. Undrawn profits are discussed further later in this chapter.

If the business is a limited company, the capital is the share capital issued to the investors in the company. Profits left in the business are called profit and loss account reserves (see Chapter 4 for more information) and there may also be other reserves. These are explained later in this chapter and company Balance Sheets are discussed further in Chapter 4.

Examples of Balance Sheets are shown in Appendices A.2, B.2 and C.3. These are discussed later in this chapter.

Explanations of the Balance Sheet headings are set out below.

Fixed assets

Fixed assets are generally used in the business over a number of years. There are two different types of fixed assets – tangible and intangible.

Most tangible fixed assets can be seen and touched. Examples are land and buildings, motor vehicles, plant and machinery, and furniture. Long-term investments, usually shares in other companies, are also tangible fixed assets.

Examples of intangible fixed assets are patents, copyrights and trademarks.

Fixed assets are usually written off over the period of their useful lives by charging depreciation. This is explained in Chapter 1.

The figure shown in the Balance Sheet for fixed assets is the written down value, which is the original cost less depreciation to date, unless there has been a revaluation. It is not necessarily the value for which the asset could be sold. Revaluations are explained later in this chapter. Details of the figures for cost and depreciation will usually be shown in a Note to the Accounts. An example of such a note, giving further details of the fixed assets figure shown in the Balance Sheet, can be seen in note 1 of Appendix A.3.

Current assets

Current assets are made up of cash and other assets that are expected to be turned into cash in the near future. Examples of current assets are:

- Cash at bank

- Cash in hand

- Short-term investments

- Stock of goods for resale, etc.
- Work-in-progress
- Debtors
- Prepayments

Cash at bank

This includes current and deposit bank accounts. Cash held in a building society is treated in the same way.

Cash in hand

This includes petty cash, as well as any cash from takings, etc., which is held before it is paid into the bank.

Short-term investments

Investments held for a short time with the intention of being sold in the near future are shown as current assets, whereas investments intended to be held for a longer time in order to produce income from dividends, etc. are classified as fixed assets.

Stock of goods for resale, etc.

In a retail business this item would be the goods ready to be sold to customers. A manufacturing business would include raw materials as well as finished goods. If there were significant stocks of consumable items, such as stationery for use in the business or spare parts for the repair of business assets, these would also be included in current assets.

Stock is valued in the Balance Sheet at the lower of cost or net realisable value. This means that if the goods are expected to be sold for more than the cost to the business, then the cost price is used, but if the sale (realisable) price is likely to be less than the cost of the goods to the business, the value used is the selling price less any additional costs that will be needed to sell the goods. If it is unlikely that the stock will ever be sold, it should not be given a value. The normal rule is that the business will only show a profit in the accounts in the period that stock has actually been sold.

Work-in-progress

In a manufacturing business there are likely to be some items that have been partly manufactured but need further work carried out before they are in a state to be sold. This is work-in-progress and, like stock, it is valued at the lower of cost or net realisable value. Cost includes the cost of raw materials and the cost of labour used in the manufacture. Cost may also include some other direct costs of manufacture, such as the electricity used to power a machine, as well as some of the business overheads.

Businesses that provide a service may also have work-in-progress. This would normally represent the cost of work that has been carried out but not completed up to the Balance Sheet date and is invoiced to the client after the Balance Sheet date when the work has been completed. Where work-in-progress takes a very long time to complete, such as a building project, it may be appropriate to include some profit as each stage is completed.

Debtors

Debtors are amounts owing to the business at the Balance Sheet date, generally for sales made to customers before the Balance Sheet date, although they may include amounts owing for any purpose. The amounts to be included in current assets are the amounts expected to be received, so if it appears unlikely that a customer will pay the full amount invoiced, the amount not expected to be received should be deducted to arrive at the debtors figure.

Prepayments

Sometimes expenses are paid in advance and may partly relate to a period after the Balance Sheet date. For example, if the Balance Sheet date is 30 September and an insurance premium is paid on 1 July one year in advance up to the following 30 June, there is a prepayment of nine months at 30 September. This is carried forward into the following accounting period by including three-quarters of the annual premium in current assets at the Balance Sheet date.

Current liabilities

Current liabilities are amounts owing by the business and payable in the near future. Where the business is a company governed by the Companies Act, the items included as current liabilities must be payable within 12 months of the Balance Sheet date. Amounts payable after more than 12 months are shown separately below the figure for net current assets or liabilities. Although there are no legal requirements for sole traders or partnerships to use the same treatment, they would normally show the figures in the same way.

Current liabilities include the following:

- Bank overdraft
- Bank loans
- Other loans
- Hire purchase
- Creditors
- Accruals

Bank overdraft

This is the amount overdrawn at the Balance Sheet date. In some cases the bank statements may show a balance in hand but, after deducting cheques drawn but not yet presented, the balance may be turned into an overdraft.

Bank loans and other loans

These include any part of a bank or other loan repayable in the next 12 months or on demand.

Hire purchase

This is the capital outstanding on hire purchase and repayable in the next 12 months. Although interest would normally be payable in the next 12 months, this is not brought into the accounts until it is actually payable.

Creditors

Creditors include any amounts owing by the business and payable in the next 12 months. They include amounts payable to suppliers for goods and services purchased before the Balance Sheet date, as well as tax and VAT payable to HM Revenue & Customs (HMRC).

Accruals

Accruals are amounts payable by the business for services received before the Balance Sheet date but not payable until after the Balance Sheet date. For example, if the Balance Sheet date is 30 September and there is a quarterly bill for electricity, if the next bill is due for the quarter ending 31 October, there will be an accrual for the cost of electricity for the two months to 30 September.

Liabilities due after more than one year

These are similar to the current liabilities but, as the heading shows, are due after more than one year. The most usual items under this heading would be bank or other loans and amounts due under hire purchase.

Provisions

On some Balance Sheets there may be a figure for provisions included immediately after the figure for liabilities due after more than one year. A provision is a liability but is shown separately from other liabilities because the timing or amount of the liability is uncertain.

A provision would be required if, for example, legal action had been taken against the business relating to an event that had happened before the end of the year and, although there was a reasonable expectation that the case would succeed and the business would be required to pay damages, there was no absolute certainty of any amount that would be payable. The provision would set aside out of the profits the estimated amount of damages that might be payable. If there was a reasonable expectation that the case would fail and no damages would be payable, there would be no requirement for a provision, but a note to the accounts would be included to explain the situation, giving the reasons why the case was expected to fail. Such a note would have the heading 'contingent liability'. This is further referred to in Chapter 4.

Capital

This is the money put into the business by the proprietor and is intended to stay in the business permanently or for a number of years. Share capital in a company is dealt with in Chapter 4.

Undrawn profits

In the accounts for a sole trader (or partnership), the undrawn profits figure is made up of the balances remaining on the proprietor's current account. A proprietor's current account consists of the following:

	£	£
Balance brought forward from previous year		*
Cash introduced		*
Business expenses paid privately		*
Share of profit for the year		*
Total credits		*
Less:		
Drawings	*	
Private proportions of business expenses	*	

Share of net loss for the year	*	
Total deductions		*
Balance carried forward at end of year		*

Cash introduced

This is money paid into the business by the proprietor that is not intended to be long-term capital. If it is intended to be long-term capital and there is a separate capital account, it may be included in the capital account instead of the current account.

Business expenses paid privately

Any business expenses paid by the proprietor and not reimbursed are credited to the proprietor's current account.

Share of profit for the year

This is the net profit transferred from the Profit and Loss Account. In a partnership it would be divided between the partners in the agreed shares. In some partnerships, partners may be entitled to a salary or interest on their capital before the balance of the net profit is divided between the partners. When this is the case, the salaries or interest on capital are also credited to the partners' current accounts, if they have not actually been paid to the partners.

Drawings

Drawings are amounts taken out of the business for personal use. They include cash, personal expenses and personal tax payments paid by the business.

Private proportions of business expenses

Some expenses paid by the business can be partly for the business and partly private. For example, when a car is owned and used by the business it is probable that the car is also used for private journeys and the private proportion of motor expenses is therefore charged to the proprietor's current account.

Share of net loss for the year

When the business has made a loss instead of a profit, the loss is deducted from the proprietor's current account.

Revaluations

The net assets of a business can be increased by:

- a net profit retained in the business;
- a payment into the business by the proprietor;
- the introduction of other long-term capital, such as the issue of shares by a company.

The net assets can be decreased by:

- a net loss;
- withdrawals from the business by the proprietor;
- the repayment of capital to shareholders;
- the payment of dividends to shareholders.

Net assets can also be increased or decreased by revaluations.

The normal rule with Balance Sheet values is that the amount shown in the Balance Sheet for current assets is the cost to the business or the net realisable amount if this is lower. For example, if stock for resale costs the business £1,000 and it can be sold for £1,500, it is included in the Balance Sheet at the cost of £1,000. If it can only be sold for £900, then the Balance Sheet value is the realisable value of £900. If, after the business had paid £1,000, the supplier increased the future price of that particular stock line to £1,100, as long as the selling price to customers is greater than £1,000 the business would still include the stock in the Balance Sheet at £1,000 – the amount it actually paid, and not the replacement cost.

The rules are different for fixed assets. Although they are usually valued at the cost to the business less depreciation to date, there is also an option to revalue. The fixed assets most likely to be revalued are land and buildings. Depreciation is then calculated on the revalued amount. The revaluation can be either up or down and the revalued amount is usually the market value based on the existing use.

Example of revaluation

A business owns land and buildings that cost £30,000. Depreciation has been charged on the buildings for a number of years and amounts to £4,000. Ignoring all other items, the Balance Sheet appears as follows:

	£
Land and buildings	
Cost	30,000
Less depreciation	4,000
Net assets	26,000
Financed by:	
Capital account	26,000

If the land and buildings are now valued at £50,000, the Balance Sheet would appear as follows:

	£
Land and buildings	
Cost	30,000
Less depreciation	4,000
	26,000
Surplus on revaluation	24,000
Revalued amount	50,000

Financed by:

Capital account	26,000
Revaluation surplus	24,000
	50,000

Although there has been no trading or other realised profit, the net assets figure has now increased by £24,000 without the introduction of any further money from the proprietor. Of course, the business has no more assets than it had before the revaluation. There is simply a different value used for an existing asset.

In a limited company, the revaluation surplus is included in a reserve account called the 'revaluation reserve'. In the accounts of a sole trader (or partnership) any revaluation surplus is usually added to the proprietor's capital account.

A revaluation surplus is an unrealised profit. A revaluation deficit (when the revalued amount is less than the original cost) is an unrealised loss. The surplus or deficit would only become a realised profit or loss when the land and buildings are actually sold for the revalued amount.

Revaluations need to be applied with caution. A revaluation surplus may improve the appearance of the Balance Sheet by increasing the value of the assets, but it does not bring in any new assets. Overvaluing assets can mislead and give a false sense of security.

There is no compulsion to revalue fixed assets, but a limited company must follow Financial Reporting Standards (see Chapter 4) and if a revaluation is included in the accounts, there must be subsequent revaluations at intervals of five years, or more frequently if there have been any significant changes in the values.

Whether there have been revaluations or not in the past, fixed assets should be reviewed each year and if their value to the business becomes less than the amount included in the Balance Sheet, consideration should be given to writing the value down to a more realistic level with additional depreciation. It can often happen that a fixed asset has a value to the business in producing or marketing a product, but it would have no value as a saleable item to an outsider. In this situation the amount included in the Balance Sheet should still be the value to the business, as long as the business is a going concern.

Going concern

Accounts are usually prepared on the going concern basis. This assumes that the business will continue to trade as a going concern for the foreseeable future. The figure shown for net assets when values are included on a going concern basis is not necessarily the amount that would be obtained if the business was sold. If the business is not considered to be a going concern, the assets would need to be valued on the basis that they will all be sold or scrapped and the proceeds used to pay the creditors. Any money left over would then be available to the proprietor.

The following table shows how items are usually valued in a Balance Sheet on a going concern basis and otherwise:

Going Concern	Not a Going Concern
Fixed assets	
Cost less depreciation to date or revalued amount less depreciation on revalued figure.	The amount that can be obtained from a sale. The asset may have little or no value outside the business or it could have additional value if it is used for a different purpose (e.g. if planning permission has been obtained).
Stock	
Normally cost or, if less than cost, the amount for which the stock can be sold.	In order to sell quickly, stock may need to be sold at less than cost. If there is unfinished stock used in a manufacturing process, it may have no value if the business does not continue.
Debtors	
The amounts expected to be received from customers.	The amounts expected to be received from customers. If the business is not continuing, the

	recovery of debts in full can sometimes be more difficult.

Cash and bank

The actual amounts.	The actual amounts.

Liabilities

The amounts owing to creditors.	The amounts owing to creditors. In some cases it may be possible to negotiate lower amounts. There are also likely to be additional liabilities (e.g. legal expenses for selling assets and liquidator's expenses).

Even if the business is sold as a going concern, the amount received from the buyer is likely to be different from the total net assets shown in the Balance Sheet. Although the price paid would probably be based on the Balance Sheet figures, it would normally be subject to negotiation and will ultimately be the amount that a buyer is prepared to pay. This could involve some revaluation of assets for the purpose of the sale and it could also involve an additional payment for goodwill if the business is successful. The valuation of goodwill would usually take into account the future expected profits of the business and such matters as regular customers, good reputation, commercial connections, good management, etc. Considerations when buying or selling a business are dealt with further in Chapter 7.

When assessing whether a business is a going concern, you need to consider whether creditors can be paid in full when they become due for payment. In the normal course of events, money is received from customers to provide the means to pay for business expenses. If creditors need to be paid before money has been received from customers, the money is likely to be provided by bank overdraft facilities, cash introduced by the proprietor or loans from other sources.

Net current assets is the key figure on the Balance Sheet when looking for an indication as to whether the business is a going concern. Current assets consist of cash and bank balances and other assets that can be turned into cash reasonably quickly (e.g. debtors and stock). The cash can then be used to pay the creditors shown under current liabilities.

If current assets are more than current liabilities (net current assets), this is an indication that the business will be able to pay its creditors as they fall due. There could, however, be a problem if it becomes difficult to sell stock or to collect money from debtors.

If current liabilities are more than current assets (net current liabilities), this is an indication that there may be a problem. It may be, however, that current liabilities include a bank overdraft or other creditor, which, although strictly payable on demand, will not be called in as long as the situation does not worsen. If the bank or other creditor is happy to continue with the existing arrangement, the business could continue to trade without repaying the bank or other creditor in the foreseeable future.

In some cases it may not be possible to continue the business unless further money is introduced. This could be an additional overdraft facility, further capital from the proprietor or loans from other sources. Selling fixed assets that are no longer required in the business could also raise additional money. Before making commitments to obtain loans, etc., it would be necessary to consider the future viability of the business. If it is unlikely that sufficient customers will be available to provide the money needed to cover business expenses and to repay the loans, it may be the right decision to stop trading.

Consider the following situation:

- Goods are purchased for £12,000 and sold for £20,000, giving a profit of £8,000.

- £20,000 is received from customers and £12,000 is paid to suppliers.

The bank account would be as follows:

	£
Received from customers	20,000
Paid to suppliers	12,000
Balance in hand	8,000

The Balance Sheet would be as follows:

Current assets	
Bank account	8,000
Financed by:	
Retained profit	8,000

Consider the same situation but this time, although £20,000 is still received from customers, the suppliers are not paid immediately. Instead, the proprietor spends £10,000 on a new car for the business.

The bank account would be as follows:

	£
Received from customers	20,000
Purchase of car	10,000
Balance in hand	10,000

The Balance Sheet would be as follows:

	£	£
Fixed assets		
Car		10,000
Current assets		
Bank account	10,000	
Current liabilities		
Creditors	12,000	
Net current liabilities		(2,000)
Total net assets		8,000
Financed by:		
Retained profit		8,000

Although the total net assets are the same as in the first situation, there are now net current liabilities of £2,000. There is insufficient money in the bank account to pay the creditors in full and, without further sales to generate more cash, it would be necessary to either sell the car or introduce further capital into the business. If there had been adequate planning, the proprietor would have obtained further capital for the business before buying the car or would have bought a cheaper car.

Chapter 5 looks at different Balance Sheet situations and gives further guidance on interpreting the figures.

Examples of Balance Sheets

A sole trader (Appendix A.2)

The Balance Sheet is considered in detail in Chapter 5, where it is used in a case study.

A partnership (Appendix B.2)

After deducting the depreciation charge for the year the net book value of tangible fixed assets is £17,192 at the end of the year. Details are shown in note 1 of Appendix B.3. Current assets consist of stock, as well as debtors and prepayments (shown in note 2 of Appendix B.3), bank deposit account and cash. The overall total of current assets is £74,750. Current liabilities, made up of creditors and accruals and a bank overdraft amount to £34,354. This figure is deducted from current assets to give net current assets of £40,396. Net current assets are added to tangible fixed assets to give total net assets of £57,588. The net assets are financed by the partners' capital and current accounts, the details of which are shown in notes 4 and 5 of Appendix B.3. Over the years the partners have put personal capital totalling £12,500 into the business as shown in note 4. Note 5 shows that drawings and goods for own use for the year were much less than the profit, leaving a total of £45,088 on current accounts remaining at the end of the year. If funds are not needed to finance the business and there is enough money in the bank account, the partners would be entitled to withdraw the balances on their current accounts. This would not affect the tax payable by the partners as the partnership profits are taxed whether they are left in the business or withdrawn.

A small company (Appendix C.3)

Tangible fixed assets have a net book value of £36,390 at the Balance Sheet date. The details are shown in note 3 of Appendix C.4. Current assets totalling £243,730 consist of stock, debtors and cash at bank and in hand. Further details of debtors are in note 4 of Appendix C.4. Creditors falling due within one year amount to £113,432 with the details shown in note 5 of Appendix C.4. Creditors falling due within one year are deducted from current assets to give net current assets of £130,298. This figure is added to the book value of tangible fixed assets to give total assets less current liabilities of £166,688. There are some further creditors of £5,209 (shown in note 6 of Appendix C.4), this time falling due after more than one year, and these are deducted from the total assets less current liabilities to give net assets of £161,479. The net assets are financed by shareholders' funds made up of issued share capital of £10,000 (detailed in note 7 of Appendix C.4) and profits retained in the company of £151,479 (detailed in note 8 of Appendix C.4). Company Balance Sheets are explained further in Chapter 4. In this case all of the issued share capital has been called up and fully paid, which is the usual situation, but occasionally the share capital is called up in instalments. If, for example, only 50 per cent of the issued share capital has been called up at the Balance Sheet date, only 50 per cent of the issued share capital, described as 'called up' share capital, will be shown on the Balance Sheet. If, at the Balance Sheet date, the shareholders have paid the full amount called up, the issued share capital is described as 'called up and fully paid'. If they have only paid part of the amount called up, the description is 'called up and partly paid'.

CHAPTER 3

The Cash Flow Statement

The Trading and Profit and Loss Account and Balance Sheet include all the transactions for the period, whether or not they involve cash. The term 'cash' in this context includes transactions through a bank account, as well as notes and coins. Although it is unlikely, it is possible for the accounts to involve no cash at all. For example, it could be that, at the end of the period, none of the customers have paid for the goods sold, none of the suppliers have been paid for the goods purchased and none of the expenses or fixed assets have been paid for. The following example shows how the accounts would appear in this situation:

Trading and Profit and Loss Account

	£
Sales	10,000
Cost of sales	7,500
Gross profit	2,500
Expenses	1,500
Net profit	1,000

Balance Sheet

	£	£
Fixed assets		500
Debtors	10,000	

Creditors	9,500	
Net current assets		500
Total net assets		1,000
Financed by:		
Accumulated profit		1,000

Creditors are amounts owing to suppliers as follows:

Cost of sales	7,500
Expenses	1,500
Fixed assets	500
	9,500

Most accounts, however, include receipts and payments in cash or cheques, etc., as well as debtors and creditors. In the above example, if all the debtors pay the amounts owed and this money is used to pay the creditors, the business will have £500 (£10,000 – £9,500) available in cash, which, together with the fixed assets of £500, will make up the total net assets. If, however, none of the debtors pay, there will be no money to pay the creditors and the business will be insolvent.

The Cash Flow Statement is designed to show only the transactions that involve the movement of cash. The net effect of cash transactions will be either an increase or decrease in the cash balance for the period.

Receipts and Payments Account

A simple type of Cash Flow Statement is the Receipts and Payments Account. A small organisation, such as a club or charity, which does not have any statutory requirement to prepare a Profit and Loss Account and Balance Sheet and does not need to measure profit, may choose to prepare a Receipts and Payments Account instead of full accounts. See also Chapter 1.

Examples of a Receipts and Payments Account are shown as Appendix G.1 (vertical format) and Appendix G.2 (horizontal format).

In the examples, all the amounts shown have actually been received or paid by the club. If any members had not paid their subscriptions at 30 June, the amounts owing would not be included in the amount of £2,800. This figure represents only subscriptions actually received during the year. There could be amounts included in the figure of £2,800 that were actually due in the previous year but were not received until the year under review. Similarly, if any expenses had been incurred but had not been paid by 30 June, these would not be included in the total expenses of £2,895. Any expenses incurred in the previous year but not paid until this year would be included in the figure of £2,895. Total receipts shown in Appendix G.1 amount to £3,749 and total expenses are £2,895. Expenses are deducted from receipts to give net receipts of £854. This is added to the cash at bank and in hand of £326 held at the beginning of the year to give cash at bank and in hand at the end of the year of £1,180. Appendix G.2 shows the same information in horizontal form so that the total receipts and opening balance are shown as equal to the total payments and closing balance. If the opening balance had been overdrawn, it would have been shown on the payments side and an overdrawn closing balance would have been shown on the receipts side.

The Receipts and Payments Account therefore shows us precisely what the movements in cash have been during the period. It does not show the profit or loss and there is no indication of amounts owing to or by the organisation at the end of the period or details of assets held, other than the bank and cash balances. Where a Receipts and Payments Account is prepared as the main financial statement, in order to give the reader a better understanding of the situation it can be helpful to also prepare a list of amounts owing by and to the organisation, together with some information about the assets held. This would not be in the form of a Balance Sheet, but is simply presented as a note attached to the Receipts and Payments Account.

As a Receipts and Payments Account does not measure profit or loss, it cannot be used for tax purposes.

Cash Flow Statement for smaller entities

Any organisation has to manage cash as part of its operations and it follows that a statement showing the movement of cash during the period can provide useful information in addition to the Profit and Loss Account and Balance Sheet. Small companies, as defined in company law, have no legal obligation to prepare a Cash Flow Statement. The Financial Reporting Standard for Smaller Entities (FRSSE) (see Chapter 4) does not require a Cash Flow Statement but suggests how one could be prepared on a voluntary basis. An example of a Cash Flow Statement prepared on the basis suggested by FRSSE is shown for a small company in Appendix F.

The example small company Cash Flow Statement shows where cash has been received from and how it has been applied to arrive at the net increase in cash for the year. The overdraft brought forward from the previous year is deducted to finish with the cash balances at the end of the year as shown in the Balance Sheet. In the previous year there was a net decrease in cash for the year, which reduced the opening cash balance to an overdraft at the end of the year.

Each line of the example small company Cash Flow Statement is explained below.

Cash generated from operations

This is the cash produced by the trading activities of the company. If the business operates entirely on a cash basis, with all sales paid for immediately, all purchases and expenses paid for immediately, with no debtors and prepayments, no creditors and accruals, no stock and no other items included in the Profit and Loss Account which did not involve cash, then the operating profit would be the same as the cash generated from operations. However, this is not usually the case and, in the small company example, adjustments are needed to convert the operating profit shown in the Profit and Loss Account into cash generated from operations. Depreciation is added back to the profit figure, as this is a non-cash item. Although depreciation was deducted in arriving at the profit, no cash was actually paid out. Similarly, the difference between opening and closing stock is eliminated as a non-cash adjustment.

The adjustment for the increase in debtors is needed to reflect the fact that cash will have been received this year in respect of opening debtors, but will not have been received for closing debtors. Similarly, an adjustment is needed for the increase in creditors as cash will have been paid during the year to opening creditors, but will not have been paid to closing creditors.

Before looking at the small company figures, the adjustments to arrive at the cash generated from operations may be more readily understood by looking at a simple example as follows:

Profit and Loss Account

	£	£
Sales		100,000
Opening stock	6,000	
Purchases	60,000	
	66,000	
Closing stock	8,000	
		58,000
Gross profit		42,000
Expenses	23,000	
Depreciation	4,000	
		27,000
Net profit		15,000

Opening debtors are £9,000 and closing debtors are £12,000.

Opening creditors are £5,000 and closing creditors are £10,000.

The cash generated from operations can be seen as follows:

Cash received

	£
Sales for the year	100,000
Less: closing debtors	12,000
	88,000
Cash received from opening debtors	9,000
Total cash received this year	97,000

Cash paid

Purchases for the year	60,000
Expenses for the year	23,000
	83,000
Less: closing creditors	10,000
	73,000
Cash paid to opening creditors	5,000
Total cash paid in the year	78,000

Summary

Total cash received in the year	97,000
Total cash paid in the year	78,000
Net cash received in the year from operations	19,000

The cash generated from operations in this example can also be calculated in a similar way to that shown in Appendix F.

	£
Operating profit	15,000
Depreciation	4,000
Increase in stocks	(2,000)
Increase in debtors	(3,000)
Increase in creditors	5,000
Cash generated from operations	19,000

The Cash Flow Statement for the small company is shown in Appendix F.

The statement begins with the operating profit of £59,442 taken from the Profit and Loss Account in Appendix C.2. The adjustments needed to convert this figure to the cash generated from operations (£47,350, shown in Appendix F) are arrived at as follows:

Depreciation for the year of £12,203 can be seen in note 3 to the accounts in Appendix C.4.

Stock, shown in the Balance Sheet in Appendix C.3, has increased by £12,875 from £115,830 last year to £128,705 this year.

Debtors, shown in the Balance Sheet in Appendix C.3, have increased by £28,742 from £78,104 last year to £106,846 this year.

Trade creditors, shown in note 5 to the accounts in Appendix C.4, have increased by £13,096 from £73,051 last year to £86,147 this year.

Creditors other than trade creditors, shown in note 5 to the accounts in Appendix C.4, consist of other creditors, taxation and social security, and accruals (obligations under finance leases and Corporation Tax, also shown in note 5 to the accounts, are dealt with below under the heading 'application of cash'). The total this year is £17,185 (£1,929 + £12,446 + £2,810) and the total last year was £12,959 (£815 + £10,519 + £1,625), giving an increase of £4,226.

All these adjustments in this section of the Cash Flow Statement are simply a convenient way to arrive at the net cash received for the trading activities of the business, which is called in the statement 'cash generated from operations'.

Cash from other sources

Cash received from any sources other than trading operations is included here. In the small company example there is interest received and proceeds from the sale of fixed assets.

Application of cash

Cash paid for any purpose other than trading operations is included here. In the small company example there is interest paid, tax paid, dividends paid, cash paid for the purchase of fixed assets and hire purchase repayments.

The tax paid of £5,000 is the amount included in creditors at the end of the previous year that has been paid during this year. The tax charge of £7,500 shown in the Profit and Loss Account this year (see Appendix C.2) is a creditor at the end of this year and will not actually be paid until the following year. It is therefore not included in the Cash Flow Statement this year as there was no cash paid out.

The purchase of fixed assets of £16,480 is the amount shown as additions to fixed assets in note 3 to the accounts (see Appendix C.4), as the whole amount was paid during the year. If any part of this amount had not been paid during the year, it would not be included in the Cash Flow Statement. If there had been fixed assets bought in the previous year but not paid for until this year, the amount paid this year would be included here.

If any of the additions during the year had been purchased under hire purchase, these would not be included as part of the purchase of fixed assets in the Cash Flow Statement. Instead, there would be an additional note in the accounts to explain that certain fixed assets had been purchased under hire purchase, and the amount would be shown in this note. The amount of capital repaid during the year would be included in the Cash Flow Statement as this is the actual cash paid out. In the small company example there are hire purchase repayments during the year of £3,086 that relate to fixed assets purchased under hire purchase in earlier years. This is only the amount of the capital repayments as the interest part of the repayments is shown separately in this section, together with bank interest paid, totalling £1,753. The amount of £3,086 paid this year for hire purchase repayments is the amount shown as payable within one year of the end of last year in note 5 of Appendix C.4.

There were dividends paid during the year of £10,000. The amount shown here is for dividends actually paid during the year, even though they may have been proposed in the previous year. It is the date of actual payment that is relevant for the Cash Flow Statement.

Cash from other sources of £2,730 is added to cash generated from operations of £47,350 to give total incoming cash for the year of £50,080. Cash paid out for all items not dealt with as part of the cash generated from operations amounted to £36,319. This is deducted from the incoming cash of £50,080 to give a net increase in cash for the year of £13,761. At the beginning of the year there was an overdraft of £5,782 and cash in hand of £200, giving a net overdrawn cash figure of £5,582. The cash position has improved by £13,761 this year, turning the opening net overdraft of £5,582 into a positive net cash figure of £8,179 at the end of the year. This figure can also be seen in the Balance Sheet in Appendix C.3, described as cash at bank and in hand.

It can be seen that the Cash Flow Statement, although set out in a different format to the Receipts and Payments Account, achieves a similar purpose. It shows the cash moving in and out of the organisation during the period and reconciles the cash position at the beginning of the period with the position at the end of the period.

Cash Flow Statement for larger companies

The Cash Flow Statement for a company preparing its accounts under the FRSSE is optional, but for most other companies there is no option as the Cash Flow Statement is a specific requirement. However, the format is not the same as that illustrated for the small company. An example of a Cash Flow Statement for a company not preparing its accounts under the FRSSE is shown in Appendix E. The figures used are the same as those for a small company, so a direct comparison can be made with the layout shown in Appendix F.

Apart from some variations in wording, the first part of the statement showing the net cash inflow from operating activities is similar in both examples. The small company example then puts all other incoming cash under the heading 'cash from other sources' and all other outgoing cash under the heading 'application of cash'. The medium company example uses the same figures but puts them under different headings according to the nature of each item. For example, payments for the purchase of fixed assets and receipts from the sale of fixed assets are put together under the heading 'capital expenditure'. Each statement concludes with the increase or decrease in cash during the period which is added to, or deducted from, the opening cash balance to give the closing cash balance. A company not preparing its accounts under the FRSSE would also include some additional notes to support the figures in the Cash Flow Statement, in particular details of the movements relating to loans.

The Cash Flow Statement is part of the picture and should not be read in isolation. The Profit and Loss Account and Balance Sheet form the main body of a set of accounts, or financial statements as they may be referred to, and the Cash Flow Statement provides some extra information that helps to provide a better understanding of the accounts as a whole.

CHAPTER 4

Company accounts

The limited company

A limited company is an entity owned by its members and managed by its directors. In small companies the members and directors are often the same people and such companies are sometimes referred to as owner-managed companies. The company exists in its own right and, although the members may change over a period of time, the company remains the same entity throughout.

A company is governed by the legal requirements of the Companies Acts and by its own internal rules set out in its Articles of Association. These set out regulations governing the way the company is managed and administered, including, for example, the procedures for appointing and dismissing directors and the organisation of the directors' and shareholders' meetings. Company law provides a model set of Articles, known as 'Table A', which the company may adopt in full or vary to suit its own needs.

There have been several Companies Acts from the 19th century onwards containing different versions of Table A. The version that applies to any company is the most recent one in force at the time the company is formed. Changes to Table A in subsequent Companies Acts do not affect a company formed under an earlier Act, unless the company chooses to adopt the changes. The Companies Act 2006 is the latest of the Companies

Acts and is fully in force by October 2008. It replaces the Companies Act 1985. Copies of UK legislation, including Companies Acts, can be obtained from the Office of Public Sector Information, whose website is www.opsi. gov.uk.

Most companies have a share capital, which represents the shareholders' investment in the company. The 'issued share capital' is the share capital actually issued to members and may be fully or partly paid. The registration documents of a company incorporated before the Companies Act 2006 show the maximum amount of share capital, decided by the company itself, that can be issued. This is the 'authorised share capital' and it may be increased if required. Companies registered after the 2006 Act do not have an authorised share capital and there is no ceiling to the amount of shares that may be issued. Companies existing before the 2006 Act can, if they wish, change their Articles to abolish any reference to authorised share capital.

The liability of the members is limited to the amount of share capital called up by the company. In other words, if a member buys 100 shares on which £1 per share has been called up, the total liability of the member is £100. If the company becomes unable to pay its debts at some future date, the member would not be required to pay any more money into the company.

Share capital can be divided into equity share capital and non-equity share capital. Non-equity shares are usually called 'preference shares' and dividends paid by the company are at a fixed rate not related to the company's profits. If the company is wound up and there is a surplus remaining after paying creditors, preference shareholders would receive a specific amount that would not vary in relation to the amount of the surplus. Equity shares are usually called 'ordinary shares' and any dividends paid are not at a fixed rate but are decided in company meetings and will depend on the profits earned and whether money needs to be retained in the company or can be distributed. In a winding up, the amount payable to ordinary shareholders would depend on the surplus available and would usually be the surplus remaining after preference shareholders have been paid their fixed amount.

Companies are either public companies (Plc) or private companies (Ltd). Public companies can offer their shares to the public but private companies are not allowed to do so. Public companies must also have a minimum amount of share capital specified by the Companies Act.

Limited by guarantee

Some companies, often charities or clubs, do not have a share capital but the liability of the members is limited by guarantee. This means that if the company becomes unable to pay its debts, the members could be required to contribute a fixed amount to the company. The amount specified is usually a very small amount and is often no more than one pound for each member. The Charities Act 2006 enables a different type of charitable body to be set up, called a 'charitable incorporated organisation'. This is similar to a company but is governed by the Charities Act rather than the Companies Act.

Company accounts

As well as preparing accounts for its own internal management purposes and for HM Revenue & Customs (HMRC), a limited company is required by law to prepare accounts for its members and for filing at Companies House. The formats and disclosures for the accounts required for members and Companies House are specified in the Companies Act. The Companies Act also requires the accounts to comply with specified accounting standards, which are issued by a body called the 'Accounting Standards Board'. The standards aim to produce consistency in company accounts and set out how particular types of transactions and other events should be reflected in the accounts. The Accounting Standards Board's website is www.frc.org.uk.

Small companies, as defined in the Companies Act, are allowed to disclose less information in their accounts than other companies. In order to qualify as a small company, two out of the following three conditions must be satisfied:

- The total turnover must be no more than £5.6 million.

- The total assets (before deducting liabilities) must be no more than £2.8 million.

- The number of employees must be no more than 50.

These figures may be increased in the future and any changes will be shown on Companies House's website at www.companieshouse.gov.uk.

Small companies can also choose to prepare their accounts in accordance with the Financial Reporting Standard for Smaller Entities (FRSSE – known to accountants as 'Frizzy'). Other companies must comply with reporting standards, including Financial Reporting Standards (FRS) and Statements of Standard Accounting Practice (SSAP). There are also International Accounting Standards (IAS) (issued by the International Accounting Standards Board, whose website is www.iasb.org) and standards issued by the Urgent Issues Task Force (UITF). Companies listed on a stock exchange need to comply with International Accounting Standards and other companies may follow a similar route in future years. Some of the International Accounting Standards mean significant changes to the way accounts are prepared and interpreted. As the International Accounting Standards are initially only compulsory for listed companies and it may be some time before other companies follow suit, they are not dealt with in this book. None of the explanations and examples that follow are based on the International Accounting Standards.

Contents of company accounts

A complete set of company accounts consists of the following:

- Directors' report
- Profit and Loss Account
- Balance Sheet
- Notes to the Accounts

Small companies preparing their accounts under FRSSE have an option to include a Cash Flow Statement, but this is not mandatory. Companies other than small companies must include a Cash Flow Statement.

In some circumstances a company may also need to produce a Statement of Total Recognised Gains and Losses and a Note of Historical Cost Profits and Losses (see page 66).

The complete set of accounts is often referred to as the Financial Statements.

An example of a set of company accounts is shown in Appendix C.

Directors' report

The directors' report for a small company must contain the following:

- Principal activities of the company and its subsidiaries and any significant changes in the activities during the year.

- Names of all the directors who served during the year.

- Directors' share options in group companies.

- Political and charitable gifts exceeding £200.

- Details of any purchase by the company of its own shares.

- Statement of the company's policy concerning the employment of disabled persons (only if there are 250 or more employees, which is not likely for a small company).

- If an audit has been carried out, a statement that the auditors are aware of all relevant audit information.

When the accounts of a company have been audited, the directors need to include a 'statement of directors' responsibilities'. This statement can be on a separate page but it is often shown as part of the directors' report. Although the statement is not strictly required if the company is exempt from an audit, it is a good idea to include it for all companies as it emphasises the fact that, even though the accounts may have been prepared by a professional accountant, it is the directors who are ultimately responsible for keeping proper records and for preparing the accounts.

Additional directors' report information for companies other than small companies

In addition to the information that a small company must include in its directors' report, companies other than small companies must also include the following:

- A fair review of the development of the business and its subsidiaries during the year and the position at the end of the year.

- Amount of any dividend payment recommended.

- Amount of transfer to reserves proposed by the directors.

- Any significant difference in the market value of land at the year end from the amount shown in the Balance Sheet.

- Details of any important post-Balance Sheet events.

- Indication of likely future developments in the business of the company and its subsidiaries.

- Indication of research and development activities of the company and its subsidiaries.

- Indication of branches outside the UK.

- Statement of arrangements for employee involvement (only if there are 250 or more employees).

Public companies are also required to disclose the company's policy and practice on the payment of creditors and listed companies need to make even further disclosures, including the company's policy on directors' remuneration.

Statutory Profit and Loss Account

A company can prepare a detailed Profit and Loss Account for its own internal management purposes in whatever format it chooses. An example is given in Appendix C.5. However, the statutory Profit and Loss Account for presentation to the members must be in the format set out in the Companies Act and it must comply with the relevant accounting standards. The Companies Act allows a choice of four possible formats. Format 1 is the most commonly used and an example is shown in Appendix C.2. An example of the same Profit and Loss Account set out as format 2 is shown in Appendix D. The other two formats, formats 3 and 4, are two-sided versions of formats 1 and 2 and are rarely used.

Format 1

The statutory Profit and Loss Account does not show details of all the expenses, although some further information is shown in the Notes to the Accounts. The first part is a summary of the trading account ending with the gross profit. Cost of sales is shown as one figure without showing the details that make it up. Other expenses are analysed between distribution (including selling) costs and administrative expenses. Interest receivable and payable are shown separately and any income from fixed asset investments and investments written off would also be disclosed. Profits or losses on the sale of fixed assets are shown separately in the statutory Profit and Loss Account, although small amounts may be included with cost of sales, distribution costs or administrative expenses, whichever is relevant.

Whereas the detailed Profit and Loss Account usually ends with the profit or loss before tax, the statutory Profit and Loss Account continues, showing the tax charge arising on the profit, or in some cases it may be a tax credit, particularly if there have been losses so that tax previously paid can be recovered.

After subtracting or adding the tax figure, the Profit and Loss Account shows the profit available for distribution to the members. It used to be the case that dividends both paid and proposed were deducted from the profit before transferring the balance to reserves. Following changes to company law, dividends are now only shown as withdrawn from reserves when they have been paid or authorised in the financial year. Dividends that are proposed before the date that the accounts are approved but have not been authorised by members during the financial year are merely shown as a note in the accounts.

Format 2

Format 2 does not show the gross profit, but there is some additional information shown for the cost of sales. Distribution costs and administrative expenses are not shown separately. These are usually included in other external charges, except for staff costs and depreciation, which are shown separately.

Continuing and Discontinued Operations and Acquisitions

A company not preparing its accounts under FRSSE has to show the split of its turnover and operating profit between continuing operations, discontinued operations and acquisitions. In most companies all the operations will be continuing (i.e. the company is carrying on the same business as the previous year). Discontinued operations arise when a significant part of the business is sold or terminated. In a group this is likely to happen if a subsidiary company is sold or stops trading. An acquisition arises if the company takes on a different type of activity, which may involve setting up a new type of business or buying a new subsidiary carrying on a different trade.

Exceptional items

Exceptional items are unusual or sizeable items that need to be disclosed in the accounts to give the reader a better understanding of the figures. Most exceptional items are included under their normal heading in the Profit and Loss Account with an explanation shown in the Notes to the Accounts. Examples are:

- Abnormal charges for bad debts.

- Redundancy costs.

- Insurance claims received for consequential loss of profits which, for example, may compensate the company for losses incurred when the business is disrupted as the result of a flood.

There are three types of exceptional items that must be shown separately in the Profit and Loss Account, which are as follows:

1. Profits or losses on the sale or termination of an operation. For example, if a company is involved in farming and hotel management, which are two significantly different types of activity, and the whole of the farming business is sold, the profit or loss on the sale of the farming business would be shown here.

2. Costs of a fundamental reorganisation or restructuring of the business.

3. Profits or losses on the disposals of fixed assets. There is an example in Appendix C.2 where the profit on disposal of fixed assets of £500 is shown in the Profit and Loss Account.

Balance Sheet

The Companies Act allows for two possible Balance Sheet formats. Format 2 is a two-sided version of format 1 and is rarely used. An example of format 1 is shown in Appendix C.3.

Most businesses, whether they are companies, sole traders or partnerships, use a similar format for the Balance Sheet and the headings are explained in Chapter 2. Some businesses that are not companies sometimes show more details of debtors and creditors on the face of the Balance Sheet, but companies usually show the details in the Notes to the Accounts.

The example Balance Sheet in Appendix C.3 shows most of the headings usually found on a company Balance Sheet. Other possible headings not illustrated in the example are listed below:

Intangible fixed assets

Shown in the Balance Sheet above tangible fixed assets.

Fixed asset investments

Shown in the Balance Sheet below tangible fixed assets.

Current asset investments

Shown in the Balance Sheet under current assets.

Provisions

Shown in the Balance Sheet below creditors due after more than one year and before the total of net assets.

Share premium account

Shown in the capital and reserves section.

Sometimes shares are issued at a premium so that, for example, £1.10 is payable for a £1 share. In this case, for each share issued, £1 is included as share capital and 10p as a share premium.

Revaluation reserve

Shown in the capital and reserves section.

Profit and loss account reserve

Shown in the capital and reserves section.

The profit and loss account reserve is the accumulation of profits retained in the company from the time it began trading. Each year some or all of the profit available after tax may be distributed to the shareholders as dividends and the balance of profit remaining is added to the profit and loss account reserve brought forward from the previous year. If the company incurs a loss during the year, this is deducted from the reserve brought forward. The balance on a profit and loss account reserve is available for distribution to shareholders.

An example of a profit and loss account reserve is shown in note 8 of Appendix C.4. The amount of £110,560 at the beginning of the year represents the accumulated retained profits for all previous years to the end of last year and can be seen in the Balance Sheet in Appendix C.3 as the profit and loss account reserve for last year. The profit for the year of £50,919 is added and the dividends of £10,000 are deducted to give the balance at the end of the year of £151,479. This will be carried forward to next year.

Other reserves

Shown in the capital and reserves section.

As well as the profit and loss account reserve, there may be other reserves for specific purposes. These are generally known as capital reserves and are not normally available for distribution to shareholders in the way that profit and loss account reserves can be distributed as dividends.

Notes to the Accounts

The Notes to the Accounts provide further information about some of the figures shown in the accounts and any additional information that may help the reader to have a better understanding of the accounts. Some of the more usual notes are shown in the example in Appendix C.4.

Other notes sometimes required, but not shown in the example, are as follows:

Post-Balance Sheet events

Sometimes there may be an event that happens after the date of the Balance Sheet but before the accounts are signed that does not affect the figures shown in the Balance Sheet, but a reader of the accounts needs to know about the event to have a proper understanding of the financial position. Examples are:

- Setting up new trading activities.
- Extending existing trading activities.
- The issue of new shares after the Balance Sheet date.

Contingent liabilities

Where there is the possibility of a liability in connection with an event that has already happened but the liability will only arise if some event happens in the future, it may be necessary to include a note in the accounts to explain the situation. For example, if legal action is being taken against the company over a matter that occurred during the year but the outcome of the case is uncertain, there would be a note of explanation. If there is certain to be a liability, the amount should be included in the accounts.

Capital commitments

Details must be shown of capital expenditure contracted for at the Balance Sheet date but not actually bought until after the Balance Sheet date.

Pension commitments

When the company has a pension scheme for employees, information needs to be included in the accounts to describe the scheme with details of the company's commitments.

In some pension schemes the pensions payable are based on the contributions paid into the scheme and the amount of pensions payable will depend on the performance of the investments purchased with the contributions. The company will not be required to pay any additional contributions into the scheme to make up for any decline in the value of the investments and, although contributions will normally be an agreed percentage of the employees' salaries, the pensions paid will not be related to salaries. Such a scheme is known as a 'defined contribution scheme'.

Other schemes, which are becoming less common, base the pension payable on the final salary of the employee immediately before retirement, depending on the number of years the employee has been in employment. Such a scheme is known as a 'defined benefit scheme'. In these schemes, the contributions are invested but if the values of the investments are insufficient to pay the expected pensions, the company may be required to pay additional contributions into the scheme. It may then be necessary to provide an amount in the accounts for the additional contributions that will be required to fund future pensions, which could have a seriously adverse effect on the profits of the company. Future pension commitments need to be considered very carefully when looking at the accounts of a company. There may also be agreements to pay pensions to directors out of future profits instead of contributing to a pension scheme and any such agreements should be disclosed in the accounts.

Interests of directors

Details of any personal interests that a director has in transactions with the company must be shown. For example, the sale of a fixed asset to a director or a loan by the company to the director must be disclosed.

Details of investments in other companies

Where the company has significant shareholdings in other companies, disclosures must be made about the shareholdings and the companies involved.

Holding company

When a company is owned by another company, details of the other company (the 'holding company') must be shown.

Security given for loans

Any security given by the company for loans and overdrafts, etc. must be disclosed.

Reconciliation of movements in shareholders' funds

This may be shown as a separate statement or as part of the notes, but it is not required by a small company applying FRSSE. Shareholders' funds (i.e. the share capital and reserves) are increased or decreased by the amount of profits or losses shown in the Profit and Loss Account, but there may also be other gains and losses not shown in the Profit and Loss Account which increase or decrease the shareholders' funds. For example, shareholders' funds are increased by a new issue of share capital or by a revaluation of fixed assets.

Example of reconciliation of movements in shareholders' funds

	This Year £	**Last Year £**
Profit for the financial year	50,000	40,000
Dividends	10,000	8,000
	40,000	32,000
Other recognised gains and losses relating to the year (revaluation of fixed assets)	15,000	–
New share capital subscribed	–	10,000
Net addition to shareholders' funds	55,000	42,000
Opening shareholders' funds	115,000	73,000
Closing shareholders' funds	170,000	115,000

Signing and filing

Although the directors are responsible for the accounts, in practice they will usually appoint an accountant to prepare them on their behalf. There is no legal requirement for the person who prepares the company's accounts to be a qualified accountant, but companies, other than exempt small companies, must appoint a qualified accountant, who is also a registered auditor, to audit the annual accounts (see page 60). For a small company to be exempt from the audit requirements it must have a turnover of £5.6 million or less and a Balance Sheet total (total assets before deducting liabilities) of £2.8 million or less. These thresholds may increase from time to time and the latest figures can be seen on Companies House's website at www.companieshouse.gov.uk. Although such companies are exempt from the legal requirement to have an audit, banks or other organisations may require an audit as a condition for providing a loan. Not all qualified accountants are registered auditors. Frequently, the accountant who prepares the accounts also carries out the audit. When this is the case, accountants must follow a code of ethics to ensure that safeguards are in place to maintain the independence of the audit.

The directors' report and accounts must be approved by the directors and presented to the members. Either a director or the secretary must sign the directors' report and a director must sign the Balance Sheet. Prior to the Companies Act 2006 there was a requirement for all companies to present their annual accounts to members at an Annual General Meeting (AGM) unless, in the case of a private company, the company had passed an elective resolution to dispense with the requirement for a meeting. Under the 2006 Act an AGM is not required by a private company, although the accounts may still be presented at a shareholders' meeting if it is requested by the members. The accounts must, however, always be sent to the members.

Filing with Registrar of Companies

Company accounts must be filed with the Registrar of Companies. The accounts are then available for inspection by the general public at Companies House. If the Registrar has not received the accounts within the specified time limits, there are automatic penalties. Prior to the 2006 Companies Act, the time limit for private companies to file accounts with the Registrar was ten months from the end of the accounting year, but the 2006 Act reduced this to nine months. The time limit for public companies was reduced in the 2006 Act from seven months to six months from the end of the accounting year.

Small and medium companies may file with the Registrar of Companies abbreviated accounts that reduce the amount of information to be disclosed. When this option is taken the full accounts must still be prepared for the members.

The annual audit

- An audit is the independent examination of, and the expression of an opinion on, the accounts. Although the main purpose of an audit is not the detection of fraud, the auditor will assess the risk that fraud may have been committed.

- A registered auditor is required to carry out the audit to approved standards and from time to time the auditor's files will be reviewed by an inspector from the Quality Assurance Directorate (QAD) to confirm that the correct procedures have been followed. The QAD is a monitoring unit set up by the Institute of Chartered Accountants in England and Wales (ICAEW). The ICAEW is one of the five professional bodies whose members may audit company accounts. The other four professional bodies, who each have their own monitoring unit are:

  - The Institute of Chartered Accountants of Scotland

  - The Institute of Chartered Accountants in Ireland

  - The Association of Chartered Certified Accountants

  - The Association of Authorised Public Accountants

- An auditor of a limited company is required to report to the shareholders whether, in his opinion, the accounts give a true and fair view of the results of the company for the year and of the position at the end of the year. He will report in accordance with the Companies Act.

- If the auditor forms the opinion that the accounts do not give a true and fair view or he is unable to form an opinion for any reason, the audit report is referred to as a 'qualified' report. In such a report the auditor will give details of any figures that he was unable to verify or any figures or statements in the accounts with which he disagrees. If the qualification in the report indicates that there is significant information in the accounts that cannot be relied on and the accounts do not give a true and fair view, there may be a number of consequences. There could be investigations by the Companies Investigation Branch of the Department for Business, Enterprise and Regulatory Reform (formerly the Department for Trade and Industry), HMRC or the Serious Fraud Office, particularly if there is any suggestion that the directors have acted improperly. There may also be difficulty in obtaining bank loans and overdrafts and anyone doing business with the company, such as customers and suppliers, may be reluctant to have any involvement with the company. If it is a public company quoted on the stock exchange, there is likely to be a downward effect on the share price and dealings in the shares may be suspended.

- Some of the work carried out in order to prepare the accounts is also useful for audit purposes. Examples are:
  - Reconciliation of bank balances with bank statements.
  - Examination of invoices for purchases and expenses.
  - Agreement of sales and purchase control accounts with lists of balances.
  - Calculation of prepayments and accruals.
- An accountant preparing annual accounts without also carrying out an audit will prepare those accounts as accurately as possible from the information provided. An auditor will usually need to carry out further work that must be recorded on his working papers. Examples are as follows:
  - Attending at the year end stocktake to observe procedures.
  - Checking stock prices and calculations on stock sheets.
  - Physically inspecting the fixed assets.
  - Sending letters to the company's debtors to confirm the amounts owing to the company.
  - Obtaining a letter from the company's bank to confirm the bank balance, and various other matters.
  - Examining deeds to property owned by the company.
- The auditor will look for evidence to support figures and explanations. This does not mean that the auditor doubts the honesty of directors and staff, unless there is good reason. He is simply carrying out the audit in accordance with the standards that he is obliged to follow.

Group accounts

When one company is a member of another company and has control over the majority of the voting rights of that other company, or has the right to appoint or remove a majority of its board of directors, the company with control is called a 'holding company' and the company being controlled is called a 'subsidiary company'. In practice, a holding company will usually have at least 51 per cent of the ordinary shares in its subsidiary, although if it holds less than 50 per cent of the shares and is able to control that company, it will need to treat it as a subsidiary in its accounts. A holding company may have any number of subsidiary companies and the holding company and all its subsidiaries are known collectively as a 'group'.

The holding company of a group must prepare group accounts, also known as 'consolidated accounts', unless it is a small-sized group or, before the implementation of the Companies Act 2006, a medium-sized group. In addition to the normal accounts prepared by the subsidiaries, the group accounts are prepared by the holding company, essentially adding together the figures from all group companies, but eliminating transactions between group companies, to produce a single group Profit and Loss Account, Balance Sheet and Cash Flow Statement. In addition, the holding company must also publish its own Balance Sheet, but it is not required to publish its own Profit and Loss Account. The holding company's own Balance Sheet will show its investment in the subsidiary companies at cost less any amounts written off.

Figures in respect of transactions between group companies are eliminated in the group accounts. For example, if sales are made by one group company to another, in respect of those items the figure for sales in the selling company's accounts is the same as the figure for purchases in the buying company's accounts. These figures will not be included in the figures for sales and purchases in the group's Profit and Loss Account, which only shows trading with customers outside the group. Similarly, where there is an amount owing by one group company to another, a debtor in one company is a creditor in the other. In the group Balance Sheet the debtor and creditor cancel each other out and are not included.

Minority interests

Sometimes a holding company may have control of a subsidiary company but it does not own all the shares. For example, it could own 80 per cent of the shares with the remaining 20 per cent owned by outside shareholders. In this case, although the whole of the group profits are shown in the Profit and Loss Account, a deduction is also shown for minority interests (i.e. the 20 per cent share of after-tax profits that belong to the outside shareholders). The resulting figure, after making this deduction, is the profit available to members of the group.

Similarly, in this example, 20 per cent of the net assets of the subsidiary belong to the minority shareholders. The group Balance Sheet shows the total net assets of all the group companies and there is then a deduction shown for minority interests, being the proportion that belongs to the minority shareholders.

Small-sized groups

Groups that are exempt under the Companies Act from preparing group accounts must include in the Notes to the Accounts further information about the subsidiaries, including the proportion of shares held in the subsidiary, the profit and the reserves. Small groups do not need to prepare group accounts if the size of the group is within the limits set out for the definition of a small company, explained earlier in this chapter.

Prior year adjustments

Occasionally, errors are discovered in the accounts of the previous year, which means that the comparative figures are misleading. It then becomes necessary to show a prior year adjustment when the accounts are prepared for the subsequent year. A prior year adjustment may also be necessary if a new accounting policy is adopted. Adopting a new accounting policy does not necessarily mean that the policy was wrong in previous years. However, to make a fair comparison with the figures in the current year, the previous year's figures need to be recalculated using the new accounting policy to see if the figures are very different from those originally shown under the old policy.

If, for example, the previous policy has been to include the wages of some employees in the cost of sales figure shown in the statutory Profit and Loss Account and the policy is changed to include those wages as administrative expenses instead of cost of sales, it would be misleading to compare the

figures in the current year, which are disclosed in accor
policy, with those of the previous year which have bee
old policy.

Where significant changes would be required to the previous ye
because of an error in the accounts or a change in accounting policy, t.
comparative figures included in the accounts for the subsequent year are
amended to show the revised comparative figures. It has to be made clear
that these figures are restated and are not the figures shown when the
accounts for the previous year were prepared. An explanation giving the
reason for the prior year adjustment must also be included in the Notes to
the Accounts.

Statement of Total Recognised Gains and Losses

Not all of a company's gains and losses are shown in the Profit and Loss
Account. The Profit and Loss Account shows gains and losses that have
been realised but not those that are unrealised. For example, when a
property is sold for an amount in excess of its book value, there is a
realised gain (an actual profit on the sale of fixed assets). When a property
is revalued but not sold there is a gain shown in the Balance Sheet (an
increase in the value of fixed assets). This gain is unrealised as the property
has not been sold and still belongs to the company and the unrealised gain,
although it is shown in the Balance Sheet, is not shown in the Profit and
Loss Account. The Statement of Total Recognised Gains and Losses brings
together all the gains and losses, whether realised or unrealised, into one
statement.

For example, a company has a profit after tax for the year of £50,000 and
has revalued its properties during the year from a cost of £600,000 to a
revalued amount of £800,000, a surplus of £200,000. The Statement of
Total Recognised Gains and Losses is as follows:

	£
Profit for the financial year	50,000
Unrealised surplus on the revaluation of properties	200,000
Total recognised gains and losses relating to the year	250,000

ote of Historical Cost Profits and Losses

The historical cost of an item included in the accounts is the actual cost of that item at the time it was acquired. In the example above, the historical cost of the property was £600,000. Most items are included in the accounts at their historical cost but there are exceptions when an item, such as property, is included at its revalued amount. In the above example, if in the following year the property is sold for £900,000, there will be a profit on the revalued amount (£800,000) of £100,000 (£900,000 – £800,000). This is the profit that will be included in the Profit and Loss Account. However, there will be a profit of £300,000 on the historical cost (£900,000 – £600,000), of which £200,000 is the realisation of the surplus on revaluation included in the Balance Sheet and shown in the Statement of Total Recognised Gains and Losses in the previous year. The Note of Historical Cost Profits and Losses is a memorandum statement to adjust the profit or loss as shown in the Profit and Loss Account to show it as if the revaluation had never been made. If we assume a trading profit before tax of £75,000, the total profit, shown in the Profit and Loss Account, will be £175,000, including the profit of £100,000 over the revalued amount arising on the sale of the property. The Note of Historical Cost Profits and Losses appears as follows:

	£
Reported profit on ordinary activities before taxation	175,000
Realisation of property revaluation gains of previous years	200,000
Historical cost profit on ordinary activities before taxation	375,000

Ratios for companies

The use of ratios when analysing accounts is explained in Chapter 5 and that chapter contains examples of ratios that can be applied to most types of businesses. This section sets out some further ratios that are relevant for companies.

Earnings per share

This is calculated by dividing the profit after tax by the number of issued shares. In the small company accounts (Appendix C) the profit after tax is £50,919 and there are 10,000 issued shares. The earnings are therefore £5.09 per share (or 509p per share), calculated by dividing the profit of £50,919 by the number of shares, 10,000. If a further 10,000 shares were issued, the earnings per share would be halved to 254.5p per share, calculated by dividing £50,919 by 20,000.

Dividends per share

This is calculated by dividing the dividends payable by the number of issued shares. In the small company accounts (Appendix C) the dividends amount to £10,000 and there are 10,000 issued shares. The dividends are therefore £1 per share.

Dividend cover

This shows the extent to which dividends are covered by the available profit. In the small company accounts (Appendix C) the profit for the year after tax is £50,919 and the dividends amount to £10,000. The dividend cover is calculated by dividing the available profit after tax by the dividends (£50,919 divided by £10,000), showing that the dividends are covered just over five times by the profit. In this case, there is a reasonable safety margin so that if, for example, profits were halved in the following year, it would still be possible to pay another dividend of £10,000 from the profits in that year. If profits dropped below £10,000 and the company still wished to pay a dividend of £10,000, it would be necessary to pay the dividends out of reserves and that is not a situation that could continue indefinitely.

Yield

In the small company accounts (Appendix C) there are 10,000 issued shares of £1 each. This means that, when the company originally issued the shares, the shareholders paid into the company £1 for each share. There are dividends payable of £1 per share, so the return in this year for each share is £1 on an investment of £1. The yield is therefore 100 per cent. The original investors in a company may achieve such a high yield as the company's profits increase but, once the company has been established and is profitable, the shares may change hands at a higher price than the original £1. For example, if the original shareholders sold their shares for £10 per share, the purchasers pay this money to the selling shareholders and not to the company and the issued share capital in the company remains at £10,000. However, as the new shareholders have paid £10 for each share, a dividend of £1 per share gives a yield to the new shareholders of ten per cent (£1 divided by £10 multiplied by 100). When shares are quoted on the stock exchange, the yields shown on the financial pages will change as the share prices change.

Price/earnings ratio

This is calculated by dividing the price of the shares by the earnings per share. In the small company example, if the price paid for the shares is £10 per share and the earnings per share, as calculated above, amount to £5.09 per share, the price/earnings ratio is just under two (£10 divided by £5.09).

Interest cover

This is a measure to show how many times interest paid is covered by profits. It is calculated by dividing the profit before interest by the interest paid. Interest is £1,753 and profit before interest is £60,172 (£58,419 + £1,753). The interest cover is therefore £60,172 divided by £1,753, giving 34.3.

If a company has a loan or overdraft on which it pays interest, the interest still has to be paid whether or not the company makes profits. The interest cover ratio shows the safety margin that the company has to enable it to pay the interest. In the example above, there is a high interest cover ratio which shows that the company should have no problems in meeting its interest obligations from profits. A low interest cover ratio, for example, if profits are only twice as much as the interest, would indicate that there is a danger that the company may not be able to meet its interest obligations unless profits are increased.

Balance Sheet gearing

This shows borrowings (loans and bank overdrafts) as a percentage of shareholders' funds. In the small company example accounts, there are obligations under finance leases of £2,600 due within one year (note 5 to the accounts in Appendix C.4) and £5,209 due after more than one year (note 6 to the accounts in Appendix C.4), giving a total of £7,809. Treating this figure as borrowings, this amounts to 4.8 per cent of the shareholders' funds (£161,479), a very low gearing. Cash at bank and in hand is sometimes netted off against borrowings for the calculation, which, in this example, would completely eliminate the borrowings, and the calculation would not be required. A high gearing (i.e. when borrowings are a high percentage of shareholders' funds) may not be a problem when profits are good and interest on the borrowings can easily be covered, but, when profits are low, a high gearing may not be a very healthy sign.

Future developments

Accounting standards are continually developing and being adapted to meet new situations and ideas. Companies listed on the stock exchange are required to comply with International Accounting Standards. Changes will be seen in the statutory Profit and Loss Account, which will incorporate a Statement of Recognised Gains and Losses and the figures shown in the statutory Balance Sheet will move towards what are considered fair values, rather than the original cost. Fair value is defined as the amount for which an asset could be exchanged, or a liability settled, between knowledgeable, willing parties in an arms-length transaction (i.e. each party acts in its own self-interest and is under no pressure from the other party). It is a complex issue, the subject of some debate in the accountancy profession, and need not be considered any further here.

Although unlisted companies will be free to adopt International Accounting Standards if they wish, it is likely that they will continue to use UK standards, including FRSSE for smaller companies for the foreseeable future. Future UK Financial Reporting Standards, however, will change to reflect many of the disclosures required by International Accounting Standards.

CHAPTER 5

Reviewing the accounts

No matter who actually prepares the accounts, those responsible for approving the accounts as proprietors, directors or committee members, etc. should always examine them carefully. The figures should be reviewed and understood before they are finalised and approved.

A number of matters can be affected by the figures in the accounts, including the following:

- The amount of tax to be paid.

- How the business is carried on in the future.

- The support given to the business by the bank or other lender.

- Credit terms available from suppliers.

- The amount paid out of the business as dividends, directors' salaries, bonuses or drawings.

- The amount for which the business may be sold.

- The attraction to new investors.

The accounts should be studied carefully and questions asked about the figures to be sure that:

- The accounts are accurate.

- The figures and their implications are understood.

- There is an understanding of what has happened in the business during the period under review.

- There is an understanding of the state of the business at the end of the period.

General points

- Each figure in the accounts should be considered and questions asked if anything is in doubt or unclear.

- The figures for all items in the accounts should be compared with the figures for the previous year. This will give an indication of the direction in which the business is moving and highlight any large fluctuations that need further investigation.

- If budgets are available for the period covered by the accounts, a comparison should be made with the actual figures. If things have not turned out as expected and there are significant variances, explanations will need to be found. Budgets are looked at in more detail in Chapter 6.

- Comparisons with any available figures for similar businesses can be useful as a measure of performance, but care should be taken to ensure that like is compared with like. This subject is explored later in this chapter and in Chapter 7.

- When monthly accounts are under review (or when the accounts are for any other short period) the latest period should be compared with the same period in the previous year. A review of month-on-month results will also give an indication of trends. The review will indicate if the business is expanding or declining and point to any seasonal fluctuations.

- Where there are several branches the figures for each branch should be compared and any results out of line should be investigated.

- Look out for items that might be expected to change in relation to each other. For example, commission paid to staff or agents based on sales might be expected to move in a similar way to sales. If sales have increased by 20 per cent, it could be reasonable to expect sales commissions to have increased by a similar percentage. There may be reasons why commissions have moved by a different percentage (e.g. a change in the rate of commission paid or some sales made on a non-commission basis), but the explanations should be understood.

A checklist for reviewing accounts can be found in Appendix H.

Individual items in the accounts are now considered in detail.

Sales

- Confirm that the sales figure is the same as that declared on the VAT returns for the period. There could be good reasons for the figures to be different, but it may be necessary to explain any differences to HM Revenue & Customs (HMRC).

- Understand the reasons for any increase or decrease from the previous year.

  Assuming there are no errors, the explanation will be one of the following:

  - Selling prices were higher or lower this year than the previous year.

  - More or fewer items were sold this year than the previous year.

  - A variety of items are sold at various prices and the mix of items sold is different this year.

  - A combination of the three points above.

  - Cash has been lost or stolen and has not been included in the sales figure.

- If the number of units sold can be easily identified, the sales figure can be checked approximately by multiplying the number of units sold by the average selling price.

- Some businesses may find it useful to calculate various sales statistics and compare them with previous periods and budgets or with available statistics for the industry as a whole. Examples of such statistics are:

- Commissions as a percentage of sales.

- Delivery charges as a percentage of sales.

- Sales per square metre, etc. (in the retail trade).

- Sales per salesperson.

Cost of sales and gross profit

When sales have gone up or down it is reasonable to expect the cost of sales to increase or decrease in a similar fashion and for the gross profit as a percentage of sales to remain constant.

Consider whether the gross profit percentage is as expected, bearing in mind the mark up on individual products. Compare with the previous year and investigate any unexplained variations.

Possible reasons for an increase or decrease in the gross profit percentage are as follows:

- The cost to the business of goods for resale has increased or decreased but the selling prices to customers have not gone up or down accordingly.

- Selling prices to customers have gone up or down with no corresponding increase or decrease in the cost of goods purchased.

- Some goods have been sold at lower than normal prices to clear stocks.

- A number of different products are sold by the business with a different gross profit percentage for each product. A different mix of products sold in one year compared with the previous year can affect the overall gross profit percentage comparisons.

- Slow moving or obsolete stocks held at the financial year end have been written down to values below their original cost.

- Stock has been lost or stolen and is not included in the year end stock valuation.

- Cash has been lost or stolen and has not been included in the sales figure.

If there are no apparent explanations for an increase or decrease in the gross profit percentage, consider the possibility that some figures in the accounts may be incorrect.

Possible errors include the following:

- Stock figures are incorrect due to:
  - Errors in calculations or additions on the stock sheets.
  - Items omitted from the stock sheets.
  - Items included more than once on the stock sheets.
  - Incorrect prices used for valuations.
- The figure for purchases of goods for resale does not include amounts paid to suppliers after the end of the year, although these goods have been sold before the end of the year and included in the sales figure.
- The figure for purchases of goods for resale does not include amounts paid to suppliers after the end of the year, although the cost of these goods is included in the stock figure at the end of the year.
- Goods sold before the end of the year but paid for by customers after the end of the year have not been included in either the sales for the year or the year end stock figures.
- Money received has been incorrectly included in the sales figure (e.g. the sale of a fixed asset).
- A payment has been incorrectly included in purchases of goods for resale (e.g. the purchase of a fixed asset).

In a business involved in engineering or construction, etc. there may be records showing the gross profit on each contract. It may be possible to add the figures together for all the contracts to arrive at the total gross profit. This should agree with the figure in the accounts for the gross profit on contracts.

It is vital that explanations are found for large fluctuations in the gross profit percentage for the following reasons:

- To ensure that the accounts are accurate.
- To manage the business effectively.
- To avoid the possibility of an HMRC enquiry.

When explanations have been found, action can be taken to amend figures if there have been errors and to make changes to the operation of the business if this seems necessary.

Explanations should be given to HMRC for significant fluctuations in the gross profit percentage at the time that the accounts and tax returns are submitted to pre-empt possible questions and a costly enquiry.

Expenses

General

Consider each expense item:

- Compare the figures with the previous year and understand the reasons for increases and decreases.
- Confirm that the figures appear to be accurate.
- Obtain a breakdown and explanation for any figure you are unsure about.

It may be possible to confirm the accuracy of some figures with very little difficulty, but others may need further investigation.

Salaries and wages

If there are very few employees, it should be possible to confirm that the figure appears to be accurate from your knowledge of the business. In other cases, any significant error in the figure might be spotted by calculating the average salary to see if it looks reasonable. Divide the total salaries by the number of employees. Remember that the figure shown in the accounts should be the gross salaries or wages before any deductions for tax, National Insurance, pension contributions, etc. The employer's share of National Insurance may sometimes be included with the salaries and wages figures, in which case the heading should be 'salaries (or wages) and National Insurance'. The employer's share of pension contributions should always be shown separately.

The employer's National Insurance and pension contributions, as a percentage of wages and salaries, are likely to be similar from one period to the next, subject to changes in the rate of contributions. Significant differences should be explained.

In the accounts of a sole trader or partnership, make sure that drawings have not been included in wages.

Rent and rates

These are figures that can usually be checked quite easily. Frequently, rent is paid quarterly and differences shown in the accounts from one year to the next could be due to either five or three quarters being included instead of four. Confirm that any prepayments and accruals have been dealt with correctly. If any part of the premises is occupied by the proprietor or a director, make sure that any private proportion of rent and rates is dealt with properly. This can be made by charging the private proportion to the proprietor's or director's current account or by making an adjustment on the tax computations sent to HMRC so that only the business proportion is allowed for tax purposes. In the case of a director, any private proportion may be treated as a benefit to be included on the director's form P11D, which is the form that employers must submit annually to HMRC showing details of all the benefits that have been paid to, or on behalf of, the directors and other employees.

As well as private use of premises owned by the business, other examples of benefits include private use of cars owned by the business and private medical insurance paid by the business on behalf of an employee. Benefits are effectively dealt with as additional salary for tax purposes. The employer may deduct the value of the benefits from the profit to claim tax relief and the employee is taxed on the value of the benefits as additional salary.

Telephone

Confirm that the correct number of periods has been included (e.g. four quarters if the accounts are for 12 months). Confirm that any prepayments and accruals have been dealt with correctly. There may also be private proportions to be dealt with in a similar fashion to private proportions of rent and rates.

Light and heat

Confirm that the correct number of periods has been included (e.g. four quarters if the accounts are for 12 months). Confirm that any prepayments and accruals have been dealt with correctly. There may also be private proportions to be dealt with in a similar fashion to private proportions of rent and rates.

Repairs and renewals

When this figure is significant, a breakdown is needed to see what is included. A fixed asset could be incorrectly included in repairs or vice versa. HMRC may require an analysis when the figures are significant.

Bad debts

The items making up the charge for bad debts should be agreed with your accountant. If there is any doubt about the recovery of a debt, it should be treated as a bad or doubtful debt and charged as an expense in the Profit and Loss Account. Doubtful debts can be deducted from profits for tax purposes if they relate to specific customers. A general bad debt provision (e.g. calculated as a percentage of total debtors) is not allowable as a tax deduction.

If, for example, debtors are £100,000 and it is decided that there should be a provision of £10,000 against bad debts, as it is estimated that ten per cent of debtors will not pay, the provision is not against specific debtors but is a general provision against all debtors. In order to obtain a more precise figure for the accounts, which will also be allowable as a deduction from profits for tax purposes, it is preferable to consider each debtor individually and prepare a list of specific debtors where there is some doubt as to whether the customer will pay all or part of the debt.

Other expenses

Review carefully, understand the reasons for fluctuations from the previous year and obtain a breakdown for larger items or any items that are not understood. If there is a significant figure for 'sundry expenses', obtain an analysis and, if appropriate, show larger items under their own heading, instead of including them in sundry expenses.

Common errors in expenses include:

- Items analysed under the wrong heading.
- The purchase of fixed assets included in the Profit and Loss Account instead of the Balance Sheet.
- Repairs included as a fixed asset on the Balance Sheet instead of being in the Profit and Loss Account.
- Creditors and accruals not included.
- Prepayments not calculated.
- Private expenses included with business expenses.
- Business expenses included as drawings in the proprietor's or director's current account instead of in the Profit and Loss Account.

Net profit or loss

Compare the net profit with the previous year. The explanations for an increase or decrease will have been obtained from the review of the gross profit and expenses.

It may also be helpful to consider further some of the expenses that may or may not have been deducted in arriving at the net profit in order to compare with previous years or with the accounts of another business. For example:

- **Wages and salaries**

  In the Profit and Loss Account for a sole trader (or partnership), the net profit is the amount available for allocation to the proprietor. If another person was employed to carry out the work instead of the proprietor, there would be an additional salary deducted before arriving at the net profit.

In a company where the directors are also the shareholders, there may be occasions when additional salaries are paid to directors as a means of allocating profits instead of paying dividends. The net profit could not then be compared with that shown in a Profit and Loss Account where profits have not been allocated in that way, unless allowances are made for the additional salaries.

In some circumstances there may be a tax advantage in paying additional salaries instead of dividends, depending on the level of company profits and the directors' personal income and tax allowances. Your accountant will advise if such considerations are relevant.

- **Rent**

  When comparing the accounts of similar businesses, it may be realistic to take into account whether business premises are rented, owned by the business or owned by the proprietor. In one business there may be a deduction for rent before arriving at the net profit, whereas in another similar business there may be no such deduction.

- **Interest**

  Interest charged in the accounts will depend on how the business is financed. For example, a business financed by bank borrowings may have considerable interest charges, whereas a business financed by the proprietor may have no interest charges at all.

In order to have a more realistic view of the net profit and to make it more comparable with other businesses, it can sometimes be convenient to show the net profit figure both before and after items such as interest. This happens in the statutory Profit and Loss Account of a company (see Chapter 4).

The company statutory Profit and Loss Account continues beyond the net profit to show the tax charged on the profits. Some of the profit remaining after tax may be allocated to shareholders by way of dividends. A partnership Profit and Loss Account will also show the allocation to partners. The allocation may be a straight division of the net profit according to the agreed split or some partners may be allocated a salary or other agreed amount before the balance of the net profit is divided between the partners. See the example of a partnership Profit and Loss Account in Appendix B.1, where a salary of £10,000 has been allocated to Partner A before the balance of profits is divided equally. In some partnerships the partners may be paid interest on the capital they have put into the business (or charged interest on overdrawn capital or current accounts) before the balance of net profit is allocated.

Consider the following example. There are two businesses with identical sales, cost of sales and gross profit as follows:

	£
Sales	100,000
Cost of sales	60,000
Gross profit	40,000

One business is a company operated by two directors and the other is a partnership operated by two partners. The company pays directors' salaries of £20,000, rent of premises of £5,000 and interest of £3,000 on a bank loan. Other expenses amount to £12,000.

In the partnership the partners receive their income as a share of the profits. The premises are owned jointly by the partners and there is no rent charged. The partnership is financed by the partners instead of using a bank loan and no interest is paid to the partners.

The Profit and Loss Account of the company is as follows:

	£	£
Sales		100,000
Cost of sales		60,000
Gross profit		40,000
Directors' salaries	20,000	
Rent	5,000	
Interest	3,000	
Other expenses	12,000	
		40,000
Net profit		NIL

The Profit and Loss Account of the partnership is as follows:

	£
Sales	100,000
Cost of sales	60,000
Gross profit	40,000
Expenses	12,000
Net profit	28,000

If you simply look at the net profit it appears that the partnership, with its profit of £28,000, has outperformed the company, which shows no profit at all. However, in order to compare the performance of each business the partnership accounts need to be adjusted to include notional partners' salaries, rent and interest so that like is being compared with like. The adjustment is just for comparison purposes and will not change the partnership accounts that are used for tax and other purposes. The partners as individuals could, if they wished, charge rent to the partnership for the use of the premises and charge interest on the capital they have put into the business. If, for example, there are three partners and the business is operated from premises owned by only one of the partners, it would be reasonable for the partner owning the premises to receive rent from the other partners. Similarly, if the partners all put different amounts of capital into the business, by charging interest to the partnership, the partners will be compensated according to the amounts of capital they have contributed.

Return on capital employed

A useful ratio to look at in connection with the net profit is return on capital employed. This ratio is an indication of the efficiency of the business, showing the profits that have been earned from the capital used in the business. Some businesses (e.g. consultancy businesses) may make large profits without the need for any significant assets, whereas others (e.g. manufacturing businesses) need a large investment in premises and equipment in order to make a profit. In a limited company the shareholders will be looking at the amount of dividends they receive as a measure of the return on their investment in the company, for which the relevant ratio is 'yield', explained in Chapter 4. When the business is a sole trader (or partnership), the return on capital employed shows the amount that the proprietor has earned from his investment in the business and the ratio can be compared with the return he might expect to obtain from any other investment.

The ratio is calculated as follows:

$$\frac{\text{Profit before interest and taxation}}{\text{Capital employed}}$$

Capital employed is made up of capital invested in the business, together with profits retained in the business. In a company, the capital employed in the business will be the share capital and reserves, including the profit and loss account reserve. For a sole trader or partnership, capital invested will normally be the proprietor's or partners' capital and current accounts. The current accounts also contain the profits retained. As the ratio is calculating the return on capital invested in the business, it is important that a sole trader or partner should also consider the effort that he has invested in the business in addition to any financial investment. Where the proprietor works in the business, the net profit is partly a reward for the work carried out in the business by the proprietor and partly a return on the capital invested in the business. Before calculating the return on capital ratio, there should be a notional amount deducted from the profit, equal to the salary that the proprietor could reasonably have expected to receive for working in the business.

Balance Sheet

The Trading and Profit and Loss Account shows how the net profit or loss for the period has been arrived at. A net profit provides the business with assets that can then be used in the business or withdrawn by the proprietor. A net loss reduces the business assets. For example:

- Sales are £50,000 of which £40,000 has been received from customers and paid into the bank. The balance of £10,000 is still owing by customers.

- Purchases and expenses are £35,000, of which £26,000 has been paid out of the bank account to suppliers and the balance of £9,000 is still owing to suppliers.

- The proprietor has withdrawn £6,000 from the business bank account.

The Profit and Loss Account appears as follows:

	£
Sales	50,000
Cost of sales and expenses	35,000
Net profit	15,000

The Balance Sheet appears as follows:

		£
Current assets		
Debtors		10,000
Bank (see below)		8,000
		18,000
Less current liabilities		
Creditors		(9,000)
Total net assets		9,000
Financed by:		
Proprietor's capital account		
Net profit		15,000
Drawings		(6,000)
		9,000
Bank account		
Sales		40,000
Expenses	26,000	
Drawings	6,000	
		32,000
Balance in hand		8,000

You can see that although the net profit is £15,000, the total net assets are only £9,000. The net assets have been reduced by £6,000 because the proprietor has withdrawn this amount from the business.

If, instead of withdrawing £6,000 from the business, the proprietor had used the money to buy a car for use in the business, the Balance Sheet would appear as follows (ignoring depreciation):

Fixed assets		
Motor car		6,000
Current assets		
Debtors	10,000	
Bank (see below)	8,000	
	18,000	
Less current liabilities		
Creditors	9,000	
Net current assets		9,000
Total net assets		15,000
Financed by:		
Proprietor's capital account		
Net profit		15,000
		15,000
Bank account		
Sales		40,000
Expenses	26,000	
Car	6,000	
		32,000
Balance in hand		8,000

In this case the net assets are the same as the net profit because, instead of withdrawing money from the business, there has simply been a transfer from one business asset (bank account) to another (fixed asset).

Net assets

The net profit may be considered as the increase in the net assets from one period to the next before taking into account money withdrawn or paid into the business by the proprietors or shareholders and excluding any revaluation of fixed assets.

You can see how this works by looking at the Balance Sheets in Appendix C.3 (a small company) and Appendix A.2 (a sole trader).

In the Balance Sheet for a small company the increase in net assets is as follows:

	£
Total net assets this year	161,479
Total net assets last year	120,560
Increase	40,919

The increase is equal to the profit after tax for the year of £50,919 shown in the Profit and Loss Account (Appendix C.2), less £10,000 allocated to shareholders by way of dividends shown in note 8 to the accounts (Appendix C.4). If there were no dividends payable, the increase in net assets would have been £50,919. The dividends have been paid out of the bank account during the year and, if they had not been paid, the cash at bank and in hand shown on the Balance Sheet in Appendix C.3 would have been £18,179 instead of £8,179.

In the Balance Sheet for a sole trader (Appendix A.2) there is a negative figure for net assets of £3,690, which is a decrease from the positive figure at the end of the previous year as follows:

	£
Total net assets this year	(3,690)
Total net assets last year	7,300
Decrease	(10,990)

The decrease is made up as follows:

	£
Net loss (Appendix A.1)	(4,640)
Withdrawn by proprietor (drawings) (note 4 to the accounts Appendix A.3)	(6,350)
Decrease in total net assets	(10,990)

If, for example, the proprietor decided to pay a further £4,000 capital into the business to buy a motor vehicle, the proprietor's capital account would increase to £9,000 and the fixed assets would increase by £4,000 to £8,140. This would, therefore, improve the net assets by £4,000 and change a negative figure of £3,690 into a positive figure of £310. However, if the proprietor put no further capital into the business but, instead, obtained an additional bank overdraft of £4,000 to buy a motor vehicle, while fixed assets would still increase by £4,000, net current liabilities would also increase by £4,000 and there would be no improvement in the net assets. An increase in an asset has been offset by an increase in a liability.

In the Balance Sheet for a partnership (Appendix B.2) there are net assets of £57,588, which is an increase of £33,123 from the previous year as follows:

	£
Total net assets this year	57,588
Total net assets last year	24,465
Increase	33,123

The increase is made up as follows:

	£
Net profit	47,142
Capital introduced by partner A	2,500
Business expenses paid privately by partner B	410
	50,052
Partners' drawings	(16,929)
Increase in total net assets	33,123

See notes 4 and 5 to the accounts in Appendix B.3 for movements on the partners' capital and current accounts.

Fixed assets

Movements in fixed assets should be reviewed to ensure that additions and disposals are correct and that depreciation has been calculated correctly. If there is a fixed asset register containing details of individual fixed assets, the totals in the fixed assets register should be agreed with the totals shown in the Balance Sheet.

Consider whether any items included in fixed assets are no longer used in the business or have been scrapped. If so, you should consider writing off any remaining book value to the Profit and Loss Account and, if the item no longer exists, the cost and depreciation to date should be removed by treating it in the same way as a disposal, but with no sale proceeds.

An example of disposals of fixed assets is shown in note 3 of Appendix C.4. As motor vehicles bought in an earlier year with an original cost of £8,000 have been sold this year, this cost is removed from fixed assets. All the depreciation that has been charged on those motor vehicles from the date they were bought, amounting to £6,000, is also removed. These motor vehicles are therefore not included in the net book value figure of £21,438 at the end of this year, as they no longer belong to the company. The net book value of the motor vehicles sold is £2,000, being the difference between the cost of £8,000 and the depreciation of £6,000. The motor vehicles were sold for £2,500 and the sale proceeds can be seen in the Cash Flow Statement in Appendix F. As the sale proceeds of £2,500 are greater than the net book value of £2,000, there is a profit on disposal of £500, which can be seen in the Profit and Loss Account Appendix C.2.

If there is freehold property in the Balance Sheet, you should consider whether the property needs to be revalued and the surplus or deficit on revaluation should be included in the accounts.

Ratios

All figures in the Balance Sheet should be compared with the previous year and explanations understood for variations. Further understanding of the accounts can often be obtained by calculating certain ratios and comparing the current year with earlier years. Comparisons with other similar businesses can also be useful. Ratios can generally only give an indication of trends and, where possible, they need to be backed up with more detailed information. Not all ratios will be relevant for every business so be selective in the ones you review.

Two of the key ratios, the gross profit percentage and return on capital employed, have been dealt with earlier in this chapter. Some further useful ratios are described below. The ratios are illustrated by examples in the case study later in this chapter.

Current ratio

$$\frac{\text{Current assets}}{\text{Current liabilities}}$$

This is an indication of the short-term solvency of the business. It shows the extent to which amounts owing by the business to short-term creditors are covered by assets that are expected to be converted into cash within the period that creditors are to be paid.

Generally the higher the ratio the better, but a very high ratio could suggest that too much money is being tied up in stock and debtors. If a high ratio is caused by a permanent large cash surplus, it might be worth considering how this could be better invested to produce income for the business or, if not required in the business, whether it might be distributed to the shareholders, etc.

If current liabilities are higher than current assets, it indicates that there may be insufficient cash available to pay creditors when they fall due, unless fixed assets (property, plant and machinery, etc.) are sold or more cash is put into the business.

Quick ratio or acid test ratio

$$\frac{\text{Current assets less stock}}{\text{Current liabilities}}$$

This is similar to the current ratio, but omits stocks from the current assets as they are usually less readily converted into cash than other current assets.

Debtor days

$$\frac{\text{Debtors}}{\text{Credit sales per day}}$$

Sales per day can be arrived at by dividing the total sales for the year by 365. When the business is registered for VAT the debtors will include VAT. The calculation should therefore be made by either adding VAT to sales or excluding VAT from debtors.

A more accurate way of calculating debtor days is to take the debtors at the end of the period and count back through the sales to find the number of days' sales that make up the debtors figure. This is particularly relevant if sales are seasonal. For example, consider the situation where total sales for the year are £120,000 and £60,000 of those sales were made in the final month of the year. Debtors at the end of the year are £30,000. If you simply look at debtors in relation to total sales for the year, it would appear that debtors represent three months' sales, £30,000 being one-quarter of £120,000. However, as sales in the final month amounted to £60,000, in reality the debtors of £30,000 only represent sales for half a month.

For another example, if debtors at the end of December amount to £30,000 and sales for the last two months of the year are as follows:

	£
December (31 days)	20,000
November (30 days)	15,000
	35,000

Then the debtors at the end of December represent 51 days, being sales for the whole of December and two-thirds of November as follows:

	£
December (31 days)	20,000
November (20 days)	10,000
	30,000

In practice, this type of calculation can be performed on debtors at the end of each month during the year as part of the regular management information.

An increase in the debtor days figure may indicate any of the following:

- Deterioration in the economic climate making debtors slower to pay.
- A problem with a major debtor who is in financial difficulties.
- A problem with credit control procedures.
- Inefficient debt collection procedures.
- Fictitious sales have been included in the accounts.
- Cash received from customers has not been recorded (because of either fraud or inefficiency).
- There have been delays in recording and banking cash received from customers.
- Sales invoices have been recorded in advance before the end of the period when the sales were not actually made until the following period (called 'window dressing' – see Chapter 7).
- Credit notes relating to sales in the current period are not processed until the following period.

A decrease in the debtor days figure may indicate any of the following:

- An improved economic climate.
- Better credit control procedures.
- Better debt collection procedures.
- The recording of sales invoices has been delayed until the following period.
- Credit notes have been issued unnecessarily in the period and will be cancelled in the next period.
- Cash received in the following period has been recorded early to make the debtors figure look better than it actually is (window dressing – see Chapter 7).

Level of stocks held (measured in days)

$$\frac{\text{Stock}}{\text{Cost of stock purchased per day}}$$

The cost of stock purchased per day can be arrived at by dividing the total cost of purchases for the year by 365. A more accurate result is likely to be obtained by taking the end of period stock figure and working back through the purchases to find the number of days purchases in the stock figure.

For example, if the end of year stock figure is £10,000 and purchases for the last 30 days amounted to £20,000, the stock can be said to represent 15 days' worth of purchases.

Another useful calculation is to compare stock levels with sales levels in order to estimate how long it might take to sell the stock. For example, if the end of year stock is £20,000, consisting entirely of goods for resale and the gross profit percentage is 20 per cent, the sales value of the stock is £25,000. It can then be calculated how long it would take to sell the stock. If, for example, sales for 30 days are estimated as £12,500, the stock represents 60 days at the selling price.

If possible, different calculations should be made for different levels of stock. Finished goods should be compared with the cost of sales. Raw materials should be compared with purchases. Work-in-progress should be compared with the time taken to make the products.

A high level of stock may indicate any of the following:

- A problem with stock obsolescence.

- Too much stock purchased or produced for the available customers.

- Fictitious items included in the stock figure.

- Overheads included in the stock value when they should have been charged as expenses in the Profit and Loss Account.

Lower stock levels may indicate any of the following:

- There has been better stock control.

- There has been understocking due to problems with suppliers, production problems or inefficient ordering.

- Items have been omitted from the stock figure.

- Deteriorating stock has been written off.

- There has been a high volume of sales towards the end of the period.

Creditor days

$$\frac{\text{Creditors}}{\text{Credit purchases per day}}$$

Purchases per day can be arrived at by dividing the total purchases for the year by 365. A more accurate way is to take the creditors at the end of the period and count back through the purchases to find the number of days' worth of purchases in the creditors figure.

For example, if creditors at the end of December amount to £16,000 and purchases for the last two months of the year are as follows:

	£
December (31 days)	10,000
November (30 days)	18,000
	28,000

Then the creditors at the end of December represent 41 days, being purchases for the whole of December and one-third of November as follows:

	£
December (31 days)	10,000
November (10 days)	6,000
	16,000

An increase in creditor days may indicate any of the following:

- There is insufficient cash available to pay creditors as they fall due.

- There has been tighter control over the management of cash.
- Payments made before the end of the period have not been recorded until the next period to show a better bank balance than is actually the case (window dressing – see Chapter 7).

A decrease in creditor days may indicate any of the following:

- There has been a change in policy to pay creditors more quickly than previously.
- Creditors have been omitted from the accounts.
- Creditors are no longer allowing credit, enforcing the payment of cash on delivery.

Case study

The case study that follows is a critical review of the sole trader's accounts (Appendix A).

Trading and Profit and Loss Account

Sales

Sales for this year increased by £10,000 from the previous year, an increase of over nine per cent, but how has this increase been achieved?

Before finding the explanation, look at the cost of sales and gross profit.

Cost of sales and gross profit

When sales have increased it is reasonable to expect the cost of sales to increase too.

However, while the sales figure increased by £10,000, cost of sales increased by £13,000 (from £77,000 to £90,000). On the face of it, additional sales of £10,000 have lost the business £3,000. The gross profit percentage (gross profit as a percentage of sales) has dropped from 30 per cent last year to 25 per cent this year. Further investigation is needed.

In some businesses it may be difficult to easily identify each individual item bought and sold, but in this case study, in order to illustrate the point, the business buys and sells a single product that can be readily identified.

The figures for last year were as follows:

	No.	£	No.	£
Sales			1,100	110,000
Cost of sales				
Opening stock (@ £65 each)	160	10,400		
Purchases (@ £65 each)	390	25,350		
(@ £75 each)	735	55,125		
	1,285	90,875		
Closing stock (@ £75 each)	185	13,875		
Total cost of sales	1,100		1,100	77,000
Gross profit				33,000

The figures show that the cost of each item increased from £65 to £75 during last year. The selling price remained unchanged at £100. This resulted in the gross profit on each item dropping from £35 to £25. With sales for the first part of the year achieving a gross profit of 35 per cent and the second part only 25 per cent, the average gross profit percentage for last year was 30 per cent.

Throughout the current year the selling price of each item was £100 at a cost of £75, giving a gross profit percentage of 25 per cent. As total sales for the current year amounted to £120,000 at £100 per item, the number of items sold this year increased by 100 to 1,200. However, in order to achieve the same total gross profit as last year (£33,000) total sales of £132,000 (1,320 items at £100 each) would have been needed, assuming a gross profit percentage of 25 per cent. (If the gross profit is £33,000, and we know that this is 25 per cent of sales, it is a simple matter to calculate the sales, in this case £132,000.)

	Actual Results Last Year	Actual Results Current Year	Needed in Current Year to Give Same Total GP as Last Year
	£	£	£
Sales	110,000	120,000	132,000
Cost of sales	77,000	90,000	99,000
Gross profit	33,000	30,000	33,000
Gross profit %	30	25	25

The cost of sales figure of £99,000 shown in the third column above is simply the difference between the sales figure of £132,000 and the gross profit figure of £33,000. Very often, if we know two out of three figures, it is an easy matter to know what the third figure should be as it is simply the difference between the other two.

Sales in the current year fell £12,000 short of the figure needed to give the same gross profit as last year.

The figures should be used constructively to decide on a course of action.

In the case study, possible action could include:

- **Increase the selling price.**

  This would improve gross profit without the need to increase the number of items sold. There could, however, be a loss of customers if they considered the new price to be too high, particularly if there is strong competition. A lower volume of sales could offset any advantage from increased prices.

- **Increase the volume of sales.**

  A number of factors would need to be considered, including:

  - Additional costs, such as advertising and sales staff.

  - Whether there are enough potential customers available. It may be necessary to cover a wider geographical area.

  - The extent of competition.

  - Any limits on the existing capacity of the business (e.g. storage space).

- The ability of suppliers to provide additional goods.
- **Find a new supplier to provide the goods more cheaply or negotiate lower prices with the existing supplier.**

If a new supplier is used, it would be necessary to confirm that the quality of the product is as good as that provided by the previous supplier, that future supplies at the right price and quantity can be maintained and that suitable credit terms can be agreed.

Expenses

Total expenses (£34,640) have increased by £8,640 from the previous year (£26,000), a percentage increase of 33.23 per cent. The major increases are as follows:

	This Year £	Last Year £	Increase £
Salaries	13,500	12,000	1,500
Rent and rates	5,000	3,750	1,250
Repairs and renewals	1,625	350	1,275
Motor expenses	1,250	975	275
Postage and telephone	950	750	200
Bad debts	1,975	150	1,825
Bank charges	3,800	1,800	2,000

In such a small business, once the major increases and decreases have been identified, there should be no difficulty in being able to confirm that the figures are correct and that there are satisfactory explanations. Breakdowns should be obtained for items such as repairs and bad debts, not only for the benefit of the business, but also so that any questions asked by HMRC can be answered.

Net loss/profit

Total expenses for the current year of £34,640 are deducted from the gross profit of £30,000 to give a net loss of £4,640, compared with a net profit of £7,000 last year. The profitability has therefore deteriorated by £11,640 (£7,000 + £4,640). This is explained by the reduction in gross profit of £3,000 and the increase in expenses of £8,640. Faced with a loss, the proprietor would need to look at achieving a better gross profit by increasing sales or margins or both, as well as reducing expenses.

The net loss for the year is transferred to the proprietor's current account, which is shown in note 4 to the accounts (Appendix A.3).

Balance Sheet

Tangible fixed assets

The details are shown in note 1 to the accounts. The proprietor should be aware of what is included in additions to fixed assets as these will be all the new and second-hand items bought during the year. It should also be confirmed that all assets bought, sold or scrapped during the year have been properly dealt with. If there are any assets no longer used in the business that have not been fully depreciated, consideration should be given to writing these items down further.

Depreciation at the beginning of the year is the total that has been charged in the Profit and Loss Account in all previous years in respect of the assets still held at the beginning of the year. For example, the motor vehicles were bought two years ago for £6,000 and this is the cost brought forward at the beginning of this year in note 1 of Appendix A.3. Depreciation was charged in each of the two years of ownership before this year at 25 per cent of the cost, being £1,500 in each year. This is the total of £3,000 brought forward at the beginning of this year. A further £1,500 depreciation has been charged this year to give total depreciation of £4,500 for the three years since the motor vehicles were bought. This will be carried forward to next year and, assuming the vehicles are not sold, a further £1,500 depreciation will be charged next year to give total depreciation at the end of next year of £6,000. As this is the same as the cost, the vehicles will be fully depreciated and will have no book value at the end of next year. However, the cost and depreciation will continue to be carried forward as long as the vehicles are owned by the business.

Depreciation provided for the year is charged in the current year Profit and Loss Account.

i.e.   Fixtures and fittings £1,160 (20 per cent of cost £5,800)

Motor vehicles £1,500 (25 per cent of cost £6,000)

As explained in Chapter 1, depreciation aims to write down the cost of fixed assets over their expected useful lives so that a fair proportion of the cost is allocated to each accounting period expected to benefit from their use. The rate of depreciation is a matter of judgement for each individual business and there are no set rates that must be used. In the example, it has been decided that fixtures and fittings are likely to have useful lives of five years, hence the depreciation rate of 20 per cent, and the useful lives of motor vehicles are estimated at four years, a depreciation rate of 25 per cent.

Stock

Stock has increased by £4,050 as follows:

Current year	
239 @ £75	£17,925
Last year	
185 @ £75	£13,875
Increase	£ 4,050

Stock usually has to be bought and paid for before it can be sold and turned back into cash. The bank balance is improved and bank interest saved if stock levels are kept no higher than is necessary to meet demand from customers.

The following calculations show how long stock is likely to be held before it is sold:

		Current Year	Last Year
A	Total number of items sold	1,200	1,100
	divide by 12 to give –		
B	Average number sold per month	100	92

| C | Number held in stock | 239 | 185 |
| D | Number of months to sell stock (C divided by B) | 2.4 | 2 |

The figures show that it will take 2.4 months to sell the items in stock at the end of the current year compared with two months to sell stock held at the end of the previous year.

As long as sales can still be fulfilled and suppliers can be relied on to provide new stock quickly when needed, cash flow will be improved if stock is kept to the lowest possible level. Assuming in this case that stock levels can be safely reduced to the equivalent of one month's sales (100 items), the cash flow advantage is as follows:

Stock at end of current year

239 @ £75 £17,925

Stock equivalent to one month's sales

100 @ £75 £7,500

Reduction in stock

139 @ £75 £10,425

The bank balance would be improved by £10,425.

However, if action is taken to increase the volume of sales in order to improve profitability, the monthly sales figure could increase above 100 items. The volume of sales may also vary at different times of the year. All these factors would need to be taken into account before deciding on the most suitable levels of stock to be held.

Debtors and prepayments

The details are shown in note 2 to the accounts in Appendix A.3.

Trade debtors at the end of the current year are £10,000 higher than at the end of the previous year. Collecting money quickly from debtors is one of the most important parts of running a business. One way of measuring how quickly the money comes in is to look at debtors in terms of 'debtor days'.

Assuming that sales are evenly spread over the year, debtor days can be calculated as follows:

1. Calculate average sales per day.

   (*Divide total sales for the year by 365.*)

2. Divide total debtors by sales per day.

   N.B. Debtors include VAT. The sales figure in the Trading Account does not include VAT. Exclude VAT from debtors when making this calculation.

The example works out like this:

		Current Year	**Last Year**
1.	Total sales	£120,000	£110,000
	Divide by 365		
	Sales per day	£329	£301
2.	Total trade debtors	£23,000	£13,000
	Less VAT	£3,425	£1,936
		£19,575	£11,064
	Divide by	£329	£301
	Debtor days	59	37

The figures show that debtors at the end of the current year represent 59 days of sales compared with 37 days at the end of last year. It is taking 22 days longer to collect money from debtors than 12 months previously. With average daily sales of £329, total sales for 22 days amount to £7,238. VAT increases the figure to £8,505. If debts had been collected in the current year as quickly as they were in the previous year, there would be an extra £8,505 in the bank account at the end of the current year.

Sales in the example are spread evenly over the year. When sales vary significantly from month to month it may be more accurate to look only at the most recent months for the debtor days calculation. For example, if sales in the last month of the year had been £20,000, the net trade debtors of £19,575 at the end of the current year would represent less than 30 days sales.

Calculations of this kind can only give approximate figures, but they indicate trends. They can be a very useful aid to management and warning signs should not be ignored.

Creditors and accruals

The details are shown in note 3 to the accounts in Appendix A.3.

Trade creditors are £5,550 higher than the previous year.

Creditor days can be calculated in a similar way to debtor days.

		Current Year	**Last Year**
1.	Total purchases	£94,050	£80,475
	Divide by 365		
	Purchases per day	£258	£220
2.	Total trade creditors	£13,550	£8,000
	Less VAT	£2,018	£1,191
		£11,532	£6,809
	Divide by	£258	£220
	Creditor days	45	31

The business is taking longer to pay creditors than in the previous year. This is one way in which cash flow can be improved and no sensible business pays out cash until it is necessary. However, delaying payment to creditors can be a dangerous game and should be played with caution. Financing the business to a considerable extent out of overdue suppliers and other creditors is unlikely to be a long-term option.

Bank overdraft

The overdraft has more than doubled to £34,805. If the bank manager has not already been in touch, he will be soon. The overdraft figure takes into account all cheques drawn by the business up to the end of the current year, including those that have not been cleared through the bank at that date. It is probable that the figure on the bank statement at the end of the current year is different to the one shown here, as the uncleared cheques will not appear on the statements until later.

As seen above, better control over stock and debtors could have improved the bank position.

Net current liabilities/assets

At the end of the current year the current liabilities exceed current assets by £7,830. At the end of the previous year, current assets were £1,300 more than current liabilities.

If all the current assets at the end of the current year were turned into cash, there would not be enough to pay all the creditors and clear the bank overdraft. A further £7,830 would be needed.

Comparing current liabilities with current assets gives an indication of the short-term solvency of the business. Ideally, current assets will exceed current liabilities. A business remains solvent if it is able to pay its debts as they become due. The business is not in a position to pay its debts as they fall due when current liabilities exceed current assets, unless payments to creditors are delayed or additional money is put into the business. It is true, of course, that where an overdraft facility has been arranged with the bank, the overdraft could continue year after year without being cleared. Nevertheless, a bank overdraft is normally still legally payable on demand and could be called in by the bank at any time, particularly if the terms are breached.

Total assets less liabilities

If all the assets, including fixed assets, realised the values shown in the Balance Sheet, they would still be £3,690 short of the amount needed to pay all the creditors and clear the bank overdraft.

This does not mean that if the business stopped trading at the end of the current year everything could be cleared by paying £3,690 into the business. Assets in the Balance Sheet have been valued on the basis that the business is a going concern, i.e. the business will continue to trade. In arriving at the values, the following assumptions have been made:

- Fixed assets will continue to be used in the business.

- All stock will be sold for at least the amount shown in the Balance Sheet.

- All debtors will pay the full amount owing as shown in the Balance Sheet.

If the business stopped trading, it is unlikely that the full Balance Sheet values would be recovered.

- Fixed assets may be of very little value to anyone else.

- In order to sell the stocks quickly, a substantial reduction in prices is probable.

- It is likely that debtors will be more difficult to collect when the business has stopped trading.

Substantially more than £3,690 would probably be needed.

The total assets less liabilities figure should not be regarded as the value for which a business could be sold. If trading stops, the value is likely to be substantially less. If the business is sold as a going concern, although the total assets less liabilities figure will be one of the factors in arriving at a price, it is by no means the only one. Profitability will be another consideration, but the deciding factor in arriving at a selling price is the amount that the buyer is prepared to pay.

Capital and current account

The capital account balance of £5,000 is the amount paid into the business by the proprietor in earlier years, probably when the business first started. It is intended that this capital be left in the business as long-term finance.

In note 4 to the accounts (Appendix A.3), the current account balance brought forward at the beginning of the year of £2,300 is the amount remaining after deducting drawings from profits earned in previous years. The figures for last year in note 4 show this as the amount carried forward at the end of last year.

The loss for the current year of £4,640 is deducted to give a negative figure of £2,340. Ideally, the proprietor would pay this amount into the business from private funds instead of taking money out as drawings. In any event, before taking out drawings, the proprietor should normally consider:

- Whether there is enough cash available in the business to cover the amount.

- Whether the money is needed in the business to finance present and future activities.

In this example the proprietor has drawn out £6,350, which is £8,690 more than the available balance. In effect, the proprietor has withdrawn the capital of £5,000 plus an additional £3,690. This could be corrected as follows:

1. The proprietor pays £8,690 into the business.

2. Drawings in the following year are at least £8,690 less than the profits earned for that year.

If the second option is chosen, there would have to be a significant improvement in the trading results for the following year to provide profits which are at least £8,690 more than the drawings. It could take more than one year to clear the current account overdrawn balance, but unless there are substantial profits and restricted drawings in future the position will get worse. In any case, the bank manager may put a stop to any further activity and, if the proprietor has given security on the overdraft, such as his home, this may be called in.

If there are no management accounts prepared during the course of the year, the proprietor may not have been aware of the loss until the accounts were prepared for the whole year and by then the drawings have already been taken out of the business and spent.

Full details of the drawings figure should be studied to confirm that no business expenses are included.

Conclusion

Understanding accounts means looking at the accounts as a whole. Taking individual figures in isolation can be misleading.

In this case study the first figure in the Trading Account is sales. The increase from the previous year looks promising, but after studying the rest of the accounts it is clear that the business has problems. The gross profit margin has dropped and overhead expenses have increased significantly. The result is a net loss for the year. The time it takes to collect money from customers has increased and, without additional cash, the business will have difficulty in paying its debts as they become due.

The net loss for the year shown in the Profit and Loss Account is £4,640, but the bank overdraft has increased by even more – £17,630 (£34,805 – £17,175). The main reasons for the deterioration in the bank balance being greater than the loss are:

- Customers are taking longer to pay.

- Stock levels have increased.

- Money has been withdrawn by the proprietor.

- Payments have been made for additions to fixed assets.

Annual accounts show what has happened during the course of a year. Regular information is essential to highlight problems at an early stage, which is where periodical management accounts come in. Prompt action can save money and it could save the business from collapse. The points looked at here in the review of annual accounts apply equally well to more frequent management accounts (see Chapter 6).

CHAPTER 6

Management accounts

Most people running small businesses are not trained accountants and so they use the services of a professional accountant to prepare the annual accounts, as well as provide advice on tax and other financial matters. This makes sense. It can be very dangerous for an unqualified person to attempt to run a business without obtaining appropriate advice. In most cases a suitably qualified person should prepare the annual accounts, but it may be possible for someone in a small business with little or no accountancy training to prepare simple management accounts during the year, leaving the professional accountant to prepare the annual accounts. This is particularly so where computerised accounting records are kept. In a very small business with a very simple accounting system it may even be possible for someone with no previous accounting knowledge to produce a basic Profit and Loss Account from manual records.

Management accounts are designed to produce financial information throughout the year in order to assist in the management of the business. They need to be accurate so as not to mislead, but they must also be produced quickly so they keep on top of events. In larger businesses they may be quite comprehensive, but even a small amount of information can be useful as long as it is accurate and up to date. Management accounts are most often prepared monthly, but they may be less frequent, such as quarterly.

Management accounts may contain a Profit and Loss Account and Balance Sheet and sometimes details of cash movements. There may also be other information, such as details of outstanding debtors and creditors and various ratios. Although the Profit and Loss Account and Balance Sheet will usually be prepared in a similar format to the annual accounts, there are no statutory requirements for the format as the management accounts are for internal use. In some cases, banks or other lenders may require regular management accounts in order to monitor the business.

Budgets

Budgets are forecasts or targets against which actual performance can be measured.

When budgets have been prepared, the Profit and Loss Account section of the management accounts may contain columns for the following figures:

- Actual figures for the period under review.

- Budget figures for the period under review.

- Variances between the actual and budget figures for the period under review.

- Actual figures for the period from the start of the year to date.

- Budget figures for the period from the start of the year to date.

- Variances between the actual and budget figures for the period from the start of the year to date.

- Actual figures for the same period in the previous year.

Budgets are set for each item of income and expenditure. They should be realistic and achievable and take into account all known conditions that are likely to exist in the period for which the budget is prepared. Where actual figures vary significantly from the budgets, explanations will need to be found and action taken if necessary.

Most businesses will begin working out their budget with the sales figure, and the cost of sales and expenses figures will follow.

Some organisations will need to start their budget with the expenses in order to establish the income required to cover those expenses. For example, a club with 100 members and an expenses budget of £20,000 will know that it must charge each member an annual subscription of £200 to cover expenses, if there is no other income.

If the budgets indicate that a business will not be profitable, there is an advance warning that action needs to be taken if the business is to survive. Before being put into operation, budgets should be carefully reviewed and amended if necessary.

When actual performance is measured against the budget it can be seen if any further action needs to be taken. Normally, once budgets have been set for the period ahead, they will not be amended further, unless there is a very significant change in circumstances.

Cash flow forecast

When budgets are prepared for the Profit and Loss Account, a cash flow forecast is often prepared at the same time. This will show the expected movement of cash in and out of the business and will include capital expenditure, loan repayments, tax payments, etc., as well as receipts and payments relating to the Profit and Loss Account. The cash flow forecast will usually show the bank balance at the end of every month and will indicate if additional funds are going to be required at any time.

Receipts and payments relating to the Profit and Loss Account will not necessarily be shown in the same period for which corresponding items are shown in the Profit and Loss Account budget. For example, if customers are expected to pay in the month following the sale, the amount shown as sales in the Profit and Loss Account budget for January will be shown as cash received in February in the cash flow forecast. The cash received figure will also include VAT, where VAT has been charged to customers.

It is a similar situation with expenses. For example, there may be a charge for electricity shown in each month of the Profit and Loss Account budget, but only four quarterly payments will be shown in the cash flow forecast.

Also, the payments in the cash flow forecast will include VAT, when this is part of the amounts payable to suppliers, unlike the Profit and Loss Account, where recoverable VAT is not included. The cash flow forecast will also include the amount payable or recoverable from HM Revenue & Customs (HMRC) for VAT and other taxes.

Items shown in the Profit and Loss Account that do not involve cash, such as depreciation, will not be shown in the cash flow forecast.

Computerised management accounts

Management accounts need to be prepared quickly in order to be of the greatest benefit. A computer system designed to keep accounting records and to prepare accounts can speed up the process of preparing accounts considerably and enable someone with limited accounting knowledge to produce accounts. Operating a computer system requires discipline and, although figures can be obtained quickly, they must be accurate to be of use. Decisions based on incorrect figures could be dangerous.

The areas where errors are most likely to occur when preparing management accounts quickly, and particularly when the computer operator is not a trained accountant, are as follows:

- Stocks
- Creditors and accruals
- Debtors and prepayments
- Analysis between revenue expenses and capital expenditure

Stocks

Stocktaking can be a very time-consuming activity and, unless there are only small amounts of stock, a full stocktake is unlikely to be carried out more than once a year. Where there are accurate stock records it may be easy to obtain a figure at the end of each month, but otherwise the stock figure can be a significant problem when preparing management accounts. It may be necessary to estimate stock or make an assumption regarding the cost of sales.

For example, if sales are £10,000 and prices are set to achieve a gross profit of 25 per cent, the trading account section of the management accounts could appear as follows:

	£
Sales	10,000
Cost of sales	7,500
Gross profit	2,500

Cost of sales is shown as a single figure without breaking it down into opening stock plus purchases less closing stock. It has simply been assumed that the gross profit on all sales will be 25 per cent, so the cost of sales must be 75 per cent of sales.

When such assumptions are made, consideration must also be given to any transactions that may affect the gross profit percentage, such as sales at reduced prices or stock lost or scrapped, etc., and the figures need to be treated with caution as they can be no more than a guide. Where the stock figure is significant and is critical to the results, it may be worth considering setting up stock records, probably computerised, so that a reliable stock figure can be used in the management accounts.

Whatever method is used to obtain a stock figure for management accounts, it is important that all stock should be physically counted at least once a year.

In some businesses it may be possible to calculate and record the cost of every sale made and, in this case, the total cost of sales for the period can be arrived at by adding together the cost of all the sales made in the period, producing a theoretical stock figure. It is, however, still necessary to count and evaluate stock periodically in order to confirm the accuracy of the calculated figures.

The theoretical stock figure, where the cost of sales has been calculated as described above, works like this:

		£
A	Opening stock	*
B	Purchases in the period	*
C	(A + B)	*
D	Cost of sales in the period	*
E	Closing stock (C – D)	*

This can be understood more clearly by looking at an example of a product costing £60, which is sold for £100. If there are five items in stock at the start of the period, a further three items are purchased and six items are sold, the figures are as follows:

	Quantity	£
Opening stock	5	300
Purchases	3	180
	8	480
Cost of sales	6	360
Closing stock	2	120

As can be seen, the stock is calculated at cost. The Trading Account for the period would be as follows:

		£
Sales	(6 @ £100)	600
Cost of sales	(6 @ £60)	360
Gross profit		240

Creditors and accruals

As management accounts need to be prepared quickly, there are likely to be invoices for purchases and expenses that have not been entered in the computer records for the period under review, as they were not received in time. Some invoices may still not have been received at all when the accounts are prepared. Any outstanding invoices relating to the period under review must be entered into the computer as creditors at the period end. If the exact amount is not known, it will need to be estimated. Some expenses, such as electricity, may only be billed quarterly, in which case an estimate for each month must be included in the management accounts and any under- or overestimate will be corrected when the bill is received.

Debtors and prepayments

All sales and any other income for the period under review are included in the management accounts, whether or not they have been invoiced at the time the accounts are prepared. Significant prepayments must also be taken into account. For example, an insurance premium paid a year in advance should be divided by 12, if monthly management accounts are prepared, and spread over the whole year instead of charging the whole amount to the month in which it is paid.

Analysis between revenue expenses and capital expenditure

This needs to be looked at carefully to make sure that no capital expenditure is included in the Profit and Loss Account instead of the Balance Sheet and vice versa. When there have been hire purchase transactions, it is essential to keep interest and capital repayments separate, and it may be advisable to consult your accountant so that the correct entries are made in the computerised accounts.

Management and annual accounts

If management accounts have been accurately prepared, the figures at the end of 12 months may be used as the basis for the annual accounts. The annual accounts should be reconciled with the management accounts for the 12 months and the differences explained to ensure that the annual accounts are accurate and, if necessary, lessons are learned for the preparation of future management accounts.

CHAPTER 7
Creative accounting

Art or science?

It is sometimes said that accountancy is an art rather than a science. Although the structure of a set of accounts generally conforms to a basic standard, figures may still be arrived at in different ways and be open to different interpretations. It is important that accounting policies are understood in order to see how figures are arrived at and that questions are asked when figures are not understood. Beware of the creative accountant.

Comparing figures

Comparing figures between different sets of accounts can often be extremely valuable. Some of the comparisons commonly made are as follows:

- The current period is compared with a previous period.

- The current period is compared with budgets for the same period.

- One business is compared with another business.

- One business is compared with a standard or average for similar businesses.

In order to be meaningful, the figures must compare like with like. If this is not the case, the results could be misleading and even harmful if the implications are not understood. When comparing the current period with a previous period, the periods should be of the same length or, where this is not possible, allowances must be made. In a seasonal business it could be important for comparisons to be made with the same time of year in the previous period. If most sales are made in December each year, a comparison between December in one year and June in another year may not be very meaningful. Comparisons could also be misleading if accounting policies have been changed. For example, if there is a policy not to provide depreciation on buildings in year 1 but the policy is changed to provide depreciation in year 2, it will be necessary to consider the difference that a depreciation charge would have made in year 1 when comparing the results for each year.

Accounting considerations when buying a business

If you are considering buying an existing business, a great deal of work is normally necessary to obtain information about the business before a price can be agreed and the contracts are signed. In most cases a professional accountant should be employed to carry out this work, but it is useful to have an awareness of some of the accounting points involved. Some of the matters to be considered are set out below.

- **Comparisons with previous years**

  If the business has been trading for some years, the accounts for the most recent period of trading should be compared with the accounts for several previous years and not just the immediately preceding year. This will show the trends over a period of time and it will indicate if there are any exceptional items that may distort the comparisons.

- **Comparisons with budgets**

  Wherever possible, past results should also be compared with budgets for the future to see if the results are likely to be maintained or improved. It should also be seen that budgets have been prepared on a sound basis using the same accounting policies as previous years.

- ## Wages, salaries and pension contributions

In the accounts of a sole trader there will be no salary for the proprietor charged in the Profit and Loss Account before arriving at the net profit. The net profit is allocated to the proprietor as a credit to his current account. Similar considerations apply to a partnership. However, in the accounts of a limited company, there may be directors' salaries charged in the Profit and Loss Account before arriving at the net profit and in an owner-managed company the directors may also be the proprietors. The salaries paid to directors may also be affected by tax considerations (it may sometimes be advantageous to pay additional salaries instead of dividends), as well as the amount of work put into the business.

In order to make a comparison with similar businesses and to arrive at a fair profit figure it may be best to decide what would be a reasonable salary for the work carried out in the business and substitute that figure for any directors' salaries shown in the original Profit and Loss Account. If the business is a sole trader (or partnership), by deducting a notional salary for the proprietor from the net profit you can make a fair comparison with a limited company's Profit and Loss Account that includes directors' salaries. Some businesses may employ a manager, while in other businesses the work of a manager is carried out by the proprietor. Fair comparisons with other businesses and with your own expectations can only be achieved if appropriate salaries are included before arriving at the net profit.

Similar considerations apply to pension contributions. In a limited company, directors' pension contributions are included in expenses and deducted before arriving at the net profit, whereas pension contributions paid for a sole trader or partner are included in drawings.

- ## Rent

When a business operates from premises that it owns, there will be no rent charged in the Profit and Loss Account for those premises, unless a notional rent is shown as an accounting adjustment. There may be some depreciation charged on the buildings, but this is unlikely to be as much as the rent that would be payable for a similar property. If you are considering buying a business but not the premises from which it operates, when looking at the net profit, you will need to consider the rent that will have to be paid for the premises.

- **Depreciation**

Depreciation is calculated to write off a fixed asset over the period of its useful life. As profit figures can be distorted by under- or overestimating the rate of depreciation, this is a figure that needs to be looked at carefully when reviewing a Profit and Loss Account.

- **Motor expenses**

When the proprietor or director uses a car owned by the business there will almost certainly be some private as well as business use. This gives rise to certain tax considerations and accounting treatment can vary according to the tax treatment. Where the business is a limited company it is likely that the total motor expenses, including private use by a director, will be shown as an expense in the Profit and Loss Account. The company is given tax relief on the total motor expenses, but the director pays tax on the private use as identified in the tax form P11D completed by the company. If the business is a sole trader or partnership, although it is possible for the total motor expenses to be charged in the Profit and Loss Account and an adjustment for private use made in the tax computations sent to HM Revenue & Customs (HMRC), it is also possible for just the business motor expenses to be charged in the Profit and Loss Account and the private proportion charged to drawings. Unless the treatment for both accounts and tax purposes is understood, the net profit may be misinterpreted.

- **Repairs**

Repairs will vary from year to year depending on the state and age of the property and equipment used in the business. When looking at the figures for repairs shown in the Profit and Loss Account, you should also consider the fixed assets. A large repairs figure could indicate that fixed assets are old and will continue to need significant repairs or early replacement. On the other hand, a large one-off repairs figure could indicate that fixed assets have been brought into good condition and will not need further repairs or replacement for some considerable time. A low repairs figure could indicate fixed assets in good condition not needing repair or, on the other hand, it could suggest that fixed assets are being neglected and, because of poor maintenance, are in need of replacement.

Profits could be overstated if repairs have been incorrectly treated as additions to fixed assets in the Balance Sheet, instead of being charged in the Profit and Loss Account. This could simply be an error or it could be a deliberate action to show a higher profit than has actually been achieved in order to obtain a higher selling price for the business. Alternatively, profits will be understated if capital items have been included with repairs in the Profit and Loss Account, instead of being included with fixed assets in the Balance Sheet.

- ## Bad debts

A large figure for bad debts in the Profit and Loss Account may simply be a one-off situation that is unlikely to be repeated in future years. A large figure year after year could indicate a weakness in credit control that needs some attention. When there is only a small charge for bad debts this could be an indication of good credit control or, alternatively, it could suggest that the basis for preparing the accounts is unrealistic and that the profits are overstated. The age of debtors shown in the Balance Sheet should be reviewed to see if there are old debts that should have been written off or provided against.

- ## Interest payable

Any charge in the Profit and Loss Account for interest will depend on how the business is financed. When funds are obtained from banks or other financial institutions there will be a charge for interest, but this may not be the case if the business is financed by the proprietor or his friends and relatives. In these situations there may be no interest charge at all or any interest charge may not be at a commercial rate. If you intend to buy a business, you will need to see how any interest payable by you in future years compares with interest charged in the accounts under the present ownership so that you can consider the likely future profits.

Group transactions

When a company is part of a group, there are often transactions with other companies in the same group. Some of these transactions may be normal trading activities. For example, company A is a wholesaler and company B is a retailer. Company A buys a product that it sells to retailing companies, including company B. In the accounts of company A, the sales figure will include the sales to company B at the full selling price. In company B the cost of sales will include purchases from company A at the amount payable, i.e. the selling price included in company A's sales. Company B then sells the product to the general public.

For example, transactions involving the group companies are as follows:

	Company A £	Company B £
Sales	100,000	130,000
Cost of sales	80,000	100,000
Gross profit	20,000	30,000

The cost of sales in company A relates to purchases from non-group suppliers. Sales by company B relate to non-group customers. The inter-company transactions are the sales in company A and the cost of sales in company B. The accounts of company A therefore show a profit of £20,000, derived from its sales to company B. Company B shows a profit of £30,000, derived from its sales of goods purchased from company A to non-group customers. The group has made a total profit on the products of £20,000 + £30,000 = £50,000.

However, consider the position if, at the end of the year, company B has not yet sold the products but is still holding them in stock.

The Profit and Loss Account for company B would appear as follows:

	£	£
Sales		-
Cost of sales		
Purchases	100,000	

Less: Closing stock	100,000
	-
Gross profit	-

The stock will be shown on the Balance Sheet of company B at a cost of £100,000. The accounts of company A will still show a profit of £20,000, but the accounts of company B will not show any profit as the products have not yet been sold. Looking at the two companies together as a single entity (the group), there is not yet any profit as no sales have been made outside the group. If group accounts were prepared, the sales of £100,000 in group A would be cancelled out by the purchases in group B and, assuming that company B has no transactions outside the group, the Profit and Loss Account would only show the cost of sales for company A as these relate to purchases from outside the group. The stock included in the group Balance Sheet would not be the amount of £100,000 shown in the Balance Sheet of company B as this includes the £20,000 profit that company A has made from its sales to company B. The cost of stock to the group was only £80,000 and this is the figure included in the group Balance Sheet.

In an extreme situation, company A could continue to manufacture products which it sells to company B for a profit, while company B simply holds the stock and never sells it outside the group. Although some information about transactions with other group companies must be shown in the accounts of company A, a reader could get a very misleading impression without also seeing the accounts of company B. There is clearly scope for manipulating transactions between companies in the same group in order to show the desired results in individual companies.

There may also be other types of transactions between group companies, including management charges. For example, there may be a head office carrying out central management functions for all the companies in the group and the costs of running the head office are apportioned to each individual company, appearing as expenses in the accounts of each separate company. One company may also lend money to another company or pay expenses on another company's behalf for which there is an amount of interest charged.

It may sometimes be difficult for an individual company to stand alone if it is taken out of a group and, for example, it needs new premises or management staff previously provided by a head office. It may also be more difficult to obtain financing as an individual company without the security provided by other group companies and favourable deals with suppliers may not be available for a smaller organisation. If you are considering buying or trading with a company that is part of an existing group, you may need to look further than the accounts of that individual company to get a true picture.

Window dressing

Window dressing involves manipulating figures or arranging affairs at the period end to make the accounts look better than they would otherwise look. Some types of window dressing may be perfectly legal but, where it has taken place, the reader of the accounts can get a misleading impression if figures are taken at their face value.

Some examples of window dressing are explained below:

- **Loan by the business**

  When the business makes a loan to another person or business, the Balance Sheet will show a debtor (the amount owing by the borrower) and the bank balance will have been reduced by the same amount. In order to boost the bank balance at the Balance Sheet date, if the borrower is connected in some way (e.g. another company in the group, a director or another business controlled by a director), arrangements could be made for the loan to be repaid just before the Balance Sheet date and restored soon afterwards. The picture at the Balance Sheet date is then different from how it would have appeared just before or just after that date.

- **Loan to the business**

  A loan to the business could be cleared just before the Balance Sheet date and restored just afterwards in order to remove the loan from the Balance Sheet temporarily.

- **Reducing trade or other creditors**

  If cheques to pay creditors are drawn before the Balance Sheet date, these creditors will not appear on the Balance Sheet and the bank balance will be reduced (or the overdraft increased). This may be the correct treatment if the cheques have actually been sent to the creditors, but if the cheques are not actually sent until some time after the Balance Sheet date, the figures shown for creditors and the bank balance may be misleading.

- **Sales brought forward**

  If sales are invoiced to customers just before the Balance Sheet date, there could be an element of window dressing if those sales have not actually been despatched. Profits will be given a boost if the goods are included in sales at the selling price, instead of remaining in stock at cost.

- **Goods not taken into stock**

  In order to keep creditors and stock to a minimum, arrangements could be made to delay a delivery into stock until the day after the Balance Sheet date.

- **Fixed asset values**

  A Balance Sheet can be given a healthier look by revaluing fixed assets. While this may be perfectly legitimate, an over-optimistic valuation can give a misleading impression. Capitalising items that should really be written off against profits or minimising depreciation can also give a misleading boost to the asset values shown in the Balance Sheet.

Off-Balance Sheet financing

Off-Balance Sheet financing aims to keep liabilities off the Balance Sheet. The principal purpose may be to make the Balance Sheet look more attractive or it may simply be the most economical way of financing the business. In recent years UK accounting standards have, to some extent, made it more difficult for a company to keep liabilities off the Balance Sheet.

Ways of using off-Balance Sheet financing include:

- Leasing property or equipment instead of buying it.
- Setting up a new company or partnership into which selected assets and liabilities can be moved.

Leasing fixed assets instead of buying them

When money is borrowed to buy a fixed asset, the asset appears on the Balance Sheet at cost less depreciation. The money borrowed, whether from the bank, finance company or other lender, appears as a liability. Interest payable on the loan is charged to the Profit and Loss Account as a deduction from the profits. Depreciation on the assets is also deducted from the profits. This is also the treatment when an asset is acquired under a finance lease or hire purchase, as the business takes on the rights and obligations of ownership of the assets.

If the asset is leased under what is known as an 'operating lease', the business does not take on the rights and obligations of ownership of the asset, which remains the property of the business providing the asset. In this case, there are no entries on the Balance Sheet for assets or loans. There is a charge to the Profit and Loss Account for rent or hire charges, but as the asset is not owned by the business it does not appear in the Balance Sheet. By the same token there is no liability shown in the Balance Sheet. The business may have an agreement, which commits it to leasing the asset for a number of future years, but this future liability does not appear in the Balance Sheet. There will simply be a note to the accounts, giving details of the future commitment to the lease payments.

Setting up a new company or partnership into which selected assets and liabilities can be moved

When a company has control over another company and is required to prepare consolidated accounts, it has to include the assets and liabilities of that other company (its subsidiary) in its consolidated accounts. However, if it owns no more than 50 per cent of the shares in that other company and it is not able to exercise control, the assets and liabilities of that other company would not normally be included in the consolidated accounts. Instead, the company owning the shares would show the cost of its investment in the other company as a single line in its Balance Sheet. Small companies are not required to prepare consolidated accounts.

If company A and company B get together to set up company C as a 50/50 joint venture, with neither company A nor company B having overall control, assets and liabilities could be moved from the Balance Sheets of companies A and B into company C. These assets and liabilities would then be shown in company C's Balance Sheet, while companies A and B would show a single line investment in their Balance Sheets.

For example, the Balance Sheets of companies A and B before the joint venture would be as follows:

	Company A £	Company B £
Fixed assets	100,000	80,000
Debtors	90,000	120,000
Creditors	(60,000)	(80,000)
Net assets	130,000	120,000
Share capital and reserves	130,000	120,000

Each company transfers fixed assets of £50,000 and creditors of £30,000 to company C to operate company C as a joint venture with neither company having overall control. The Balance Sheets now appear as follows:

	Company A £	Company B £	Company C £
Fixed assets	50,000	30,000	100,000
Investment	20,000	20,000	-
Debtors	90,000	120,000	-
Creditors	(30,000)	(50,000)	(60,000)
Net assets	130,000	120,000	40,000
Share capital and reserves	130,000	120,000	40,000

The investment of £20,000 by company A and company B is the net amount invested in company C by each company, being the difference between the fixed assets of £50,000 and the creditors of £30,000 that each company has transferred into company C.

If company C obtained a bank loan with security provided by companies A and B, details of the security given would need to be disclosed in the Notes to the Accounts of companies A and B, but the loan itself would be shown in the Balance Sheet of company C.

Revenue recognition

When you buy an item in a shop, hand over the cash and then take the item away, it is clear that a sale has taken place at that time. If you are allowed to take the item away with an agreement to pay at a later date, it is still reasonably clear that a sale has taken place at the time the item was taken away. If a Balance Sheet is prepared for the shop immediately after the sale, in the first case the cash paid would be included in the Balance Sheet under current assets as cash in hand and, in the second case, the amount owing would be included in the Balance Sheet under current assets as a debtor. However, what if the sale price includes an agreement to carry out maintenance during the next year on the item sold? The maintenance has not yet been carried out so is it correct to treat that part of the sale price as a sale immediately or should it only be treated as a sale when the maintenance is actually carried out?

What if you are a wholesaler and you sell goods to retailers on a sale or return basis? As the goods may be returned to you if they are not sold by the retailer, should you wait until the retailer has sold the goods before treating it as a sale in your own accounts?

What if you are a shopkeeper and you sell an item to a car mechanic who agrees to service your car instead of paying for the goods? As no cash changes hands, has there actually been a sale at all or, if so, at what time does the sale take place and is this the same time for both you and the mechanic?

Difficulties can sometimes arise in defining when or if a sale has taken place. As accounts are prepared for specific periods (e.g. a year), it is important that when a sale has taken place it is recorded in the correct period. There are usually costs associated with a sale (e.g. the cost to the business of the item sold or labour costs when a service is provided). Profit and loss figures will be distorted if the costs associated with a sale are not shown in the accounts in the same period as the sale itself.

Revenue recognition is the accounting term used when deciding whether or when a sale or other income should be included in the accounts. Sometimes goods may legally belong to one party, but for accounts purposes they are treated as belonging to another party because this more fairly reflects the nature of the transaction. Some examples of matters needing further thought are shown below:

- **Sale or return**

    Business A transfers a product to business B. Business B is required to pay business A for the product if it is sold to a third party. If it has not been sold within a set period, business B must pay business A for the product or return it.

    In this situation, the product remains the stock of business A until business B has sold it to a third party. At that point both business A and business B would record a sale (business A to business B and business B to the third party). If it has not been sold by business B at the end of the set period, the product is returned to business A and no business records a sale. The accounts of business A could be misleading if sales were recorded as soon as the goods were despatched to business B. If business B failed to sell the goods to a third party and returned them to business A, the sales that had initially been recorded in business A would have to be reversed. In an extreme situation, if no goods at all were sold to third parties, business A could show a gross profit in month 1 when the goods were despatched, but a gross loss of the same amount in month 2 when they were returned.

- **Consignment stock**

    A similar situation to sale or return occurs with consignment stock transactions between a manufacturer and a dealer, a method of trading often used in the motor trade. A dealer may hold stock on behalf of the manufacturer until it is sold to a third party or it is returned to the manufacturer. In some cases the stock may be included in the manufacturer's Balance Sheet, but in other cases it is included in the dealer's Balance Sheet, depending on the arrangements, rights and obligations between the two businesses.

- **Sales with rights of return**

Sometimes when a sale is made, the buyer is given the right to return the goods within a set period of time for any reason at all. Many retailers offer this right so that you may return the goods within 14 days, for example, simply because you decide that you do not like the colour. In this case the retailer would normally record the sale at the time you buy the goods, but make some allowance for the possibility that some customers may make returns. The allowance would generally depend on the past record of returns. For example, if over a period of time it is found that, on average, ten per cent of goods are normally returned, the retailer might consider it prudent to reduce the sales figure by ten per cent in the accounts in order to allow for the likely return of some of the goods sold. If no such allowance is made, the accounts could show a misleadingly high sales figure. Any allowance against sales would need to be kept under constant review and any percentage reduction would be amended up or down if the situation changed. A new business would not, of course, have a history to follow and so it would need to make estimates initially and adjust them, if necessary, as a trend developed. If it is impossible to make a reasonable estimate of the likely returns, then it would not be prudent to take credit for any of the sales until the time allowed for returning the goods has expired. For example, if goods can be returned within 14 days of purchase, any goods sold in the last 14 days of the period for which accounts are prepared would not be included as sales in the Profit and Loss Account until the following period when the period for returns has expired. Any cash received for those sales before the end of the period are payments received in advance and would be included as part of creditors at the Balance Sheet date. If the time allowed for returning goods is quite short (e.g. 14 days), then the actual figure for goods returned in that period is likely to be known by the time the accounts are prepared and sales can therefore be reduced by the actual returns, instead of using an estimate.

- **Turnover as principal or as agent**

Where a business acts as an agent on behalf of another business and receives a commission for arranging sales for that other business, the turnover shown in the agent's accounts is normally the commission receivable and not the sales value of the product itself. Sales of the product would be shown in the principal's accounts, the principal being the business that is ultimately responsible to the customer for the product.

- ## Maintenance services

  Some products are sold with an agreement to maintain that product for a future period. For example, the supplier of computer software may include in the price a charge for providing support and upgrades for a future period, which may be a number of years. Indeed, the major part of the price charged may relate to the future maintenance of that software. In this case, it would not be reasonable to treat the full amount as a sale immediately, as the cost in providing support and updates would not be incurred until later. It is therefore fair to spread the sale over the period of the contract. A similar situation arises if, for example, an agreement is sold to service a central heating system for the next three years. Although the full amount may be payable immediately, it should be spread over the accounts for the next three years so that the sales figures are shown in the same period as the cost of providing the service.

- ## Bartering

  Occasionally, instead of paying for goods in cash, the old-fashioned system of bartering comes into play. The farmer provides produce to the mechanic who repairs his tractor; the accountant provides accountancy services to the painter who paints his office. In each case, although no cash has changed hands, there has been a transaction that should be reflected in the accounts of each business, and a fair value, based on normal selling prices, should be established. In the case of the farmer, there is a sale of produce and the expense of tractor repairs. The mechanic's turnover includes the work done for the farmer and the equivalent value of the produce is reflected in his drawings. The accountant has fees received as part of his income and the equivalent value in expenses for office maintenance. The painter has income for his work done in the accountant's office and the accountancy fees as an expense.

Conclusion

So is accountancy an art or a science? It could probably be said to be both. Accounts have a structured format and there are rules laid down on their preparation and presentation. Formal accounting standards have developed considerably over the years for company accounts, eliminating some of the scope for disguise and making more disclosures a requirement rather than an option. However, there can still be an element of judgement needed to arrive at some of the figures and creativity amongst accountants is still not entirely unknown. The lesson is to look at the broad picture and ask questions if anything is not clear. A Balance Sheet may show a healthy bank balance, but you also need to look at the creditors, as payments could be due tomorrow which would then clean out the bank account. Sales may look good, but if they relate to maintenance agreements for the future, then next year could show heavy costs and little income.

Accounts are essential to any business and many other organisations. Used properly they tell us what happened in the past, where we stand in the present, and guide us for the future. The key is to understand them.

Appendices

Appendix A.1 Sole trader Profit and Loss Account

A Sole Trader

Trading and Profit and Loss Account for the Year Ended 30 September

	This Year		Last Year	
	£	£	£	£
Sales		120,000		110,000
Cost of sales				
Opening stock	13,875		10,400	
Purchases	94,050		80,475	
	107,925		90,875	
Closing stock	17,925		13,875	
		90,000		77,000
Gross profit	(25%)	30,000	(30%)	33,000
Expenses				
Salaries	13,500		12,000	
Rent and rates	5,000		3,750	
Insurance	650		600	
Heat and light	1,275		1,100	
Repairs and renewals	1,625		350	
Motor expenses	1,250		975	
Entertaining	380		475	
Printing and stationery	425		500	
Postage and telephone	950		750	
Accountancy	875		825	
Sundries	275		225	
Bad debts	1,975		150	
Bank charges and interest	3,800		1,800	
Depreciation				
Fixtures & fittings	1,160		1,000	
Motor vehicles	1,500		1,500	
		34,640		26,000
Net (loss)/profit for the year		(4,640)		7,000

Appendix A.2 Sole trader Balance Sheet

<u>A Sole Trader</u>

<u>Balance Sheet as at 30 September</u>

	This Year		Last Year	
	£	£	£	£
Tangible fixed assets (Note 1)		4,140		6,000
Current assets				
Stock	17,925		13,875	
Debtors and prepayments (Note 2)	24,500		14,000	
Cash	100		100	
	42,525		27,975	
Current liabilities				
Creditors and accruals (Note 3)	15,550		9,500	
Bank overdraft	34,805		17,175	
	50,355		26,675	
Net current (liabilities)/assets		(7,830)		1,300
Total assets less liabilities		(3,690)		7,300
Financed by:				
Capital account		5,000		5,000
Current account (Note 4)		(8,690)		2,300
		(3,690)		7,300

Appendix A.3 Sole trader Notes to the Accounts

<u>A Sole Trader</u>

<u>Notes to the Accounts</u>

<u>30 September</u>

1. Tangible fixed assets

	Total £	Fixtures & Fittings £	Motor Vehicles £
Cost			
At 1 October beginning of this year	11,000	5,000	6,000
Additions	800	800	-
At 30 September end of this year	11,800	5,800	6,000
Depreciation			
At 1 October beginning of this year	5,000	2,000	3,000
Provided for the year	2,660	1,160	1,500
At 30 September end of this year	7,660	3,160	4,500
Net book amount			
At 30 September (this year)	4,140	2,640	1,500
At 30 September (last year)	6,000	3,000	3,000

2. Debtors and prepayments

	This Year £	Last Year £
Trade debtors	23,000	13,000
Prepayments	1,500	1,000
	24,500	14,000

Appendix A.3 Sole trader Notes to the Accounts (continued)

3. Creditors

	This Year £	Last Year £
Trade creditors	13,550	8,000
VAT	1,200	900
Accruals	800	600
	15,550	9,500

4. Current account

	This Year £	Last Year £
At 1 October	2,300	4,800
(Loss)/profit for the year	(4,640)	7,000
	(2,340)	11,800
Drawings	(6,350)	(9,500)
At 30 September	(8,690)	2,300

Appendix B.1 Partnership Profit and Loss Account

A Partnership

Trading and Profit and Loss Account for the Year Ended 31 March

	This Year £	This Year £	Last Year £	Last Year £
Sales		409,337		346,494
Goods for own use		2,000		-
		411,337		346,494
Cost of sales				
Purchases	303,260		271,233	
Stock decrease/(increase)	2,550		(3,685)	
		305,810		267,548
Gross profit		105,527		78,946
Other income				
Discount received	2,074		845	
Bank interest received	56		-	
		2,130		845
		107,657		79,791
Less: Expenses				
Establishment	9,657		7,394	
Selling and distribution	30,998		24,598	
Administration	14,944		12,985	
Financial	4,916		7,664	
		60,515		52,641
Net profit for the year		47,142		27,150

Allocated:

	Salary £		Balance of Profit £	Total This Year £	Total Last Year £
Partner A	10,000	50%	18,571	28,571	13,575
Partner B	-	50%	18,571	18,571	13,575
	10,000		37,142	47,142	27,150

Appendix B.1 Partnership Profit and Loss Account (continued)

A Partnership

Trading and Profit and Loss Account for the Year Ended 31 March

Details of Expenses

	This Year £	Last Year £
Establishment		
Rent	4,875	4,400
Rates	1,249	1,062
Heat and light	1,273	1,183
Repairs and renewals	2,260	749
	9,657	7,394
Selling and distribution		
Salaries	13,572	10,615
Advertising	1,621	1,522
Motor and travelling	8,305	7,261
Depreciation – motor vehicles	7,500	5,200
	30,998	24,598
Administration		
Salaries	8,765	7,915
Printing and stationery	1,163	982
Telephone	1,348	1,195
Insurance	715	520
Accountancy	950	850
Legal and professional	250	175
Sundries	485	128
Depreciation – fixtures & fittings	1,268	1,220
	14,944	12,985
Financial		
Discount allowed	1,993	1,234
Bad debts	1,394	1,750
Bank charges and interest	1,529	4,680
	4,916	7,664

Appendix B.2 Partnership Balance Sheet

<u>A Partnership</u>

<u>Balance Sheet as at 31 March</u>

	This Year £	This Year £	Last Year £	Last Year £
Tangible fixed assets				
(Note 1)		17,192		17,960
Current assets				
Stock	28,700		31,250	
Debtors and prepayments (Note 2)	44,980		33,464	
Bank deposit account	1,056		-	
Cash	14		10	
	74,750		64,724	
Current liabilities				
Creditors and accruals (Note 3)	33,232		28,678	
Bank overdraft	1,122		29,541	
	34,354		58,219	
Net current assets		40,396		6,505
Total net assets		57,588		24,465
Financed by:				
Partners' capital accounts (Note 4)		12,500		10,000
Partners' current accounts (Note 5)		45,088		14,465
		57,588		24,465

Appendix B.3 Partnership Notes to the Accounts

A Partnership

Notes to the Accounts

31 March

1. Tangible fixed assets

	Total £	Fixtures & Fittings £	Motor Vehicles £
Cost			
At beginning of year	30,450	8,450	22,000
Additions	8,000	-	8,000
At end of year	38,450	8,450	30,000
Depreciation			
At beginning of year	12,490	2,490	10,000
Provided for the year	8,768	1,268	7,500
At end of year	21,258	3,758	17,500
Net book value			
At end of year	17,192	4,692	12,500
At end of last year	17,960	5,960	12,000

2. Debtors and prepayments

	This Year £	Last Year £
Trade debtors	46,450	34,964
Less provision for doubtful debts	(1,845)	(1,750)
	44,605	33,214
Prepayments	375	250
	44,980	33,464

Appendix B.3 Partnership Notes to the Accounts (continued)

3. Creditors and accruals

	This Year £	Last Year £
Trade creditors	24,047	22,719
Other creditors	1,719	815
PAYE and National Insurance	906	723
VAT	5,740	3,796
Accruals	820	625
	33,232	28,678

4. Partners' capital accounts

	Total £	Partner A £	Partner B £
At beginning of year	10,000	5,000	5,000
Capital introduced	2,500	2,500	-
At end of year	12,500	7,500	5,000

5. Partners' current accounts

	Total £	Partner A £	Partner B £
At beginning of year	14,465	8,840	5,625
Business expenses paid privately	410	-	410
Profit for the year	47,142	28,571	18,571
	62,017	37,411	24,606
Less: Drawings	(14,929)	(8,437)	(6,492)
Goods for own use	(2,000)	(2,000)	-
	45,088	26,974	18,114

Appendix C.1 Small company directors' report

<u>A Small Company</u>

<u>Directors' Report for the Year Ended 30 September</u>

The directors present their report and accounts for the year ended 30 September.

Statement of directors' responsibilities

Company law requires the directors to prepare accounts for each financial year which give a true and fair view of the state of affairs of the company and of the profit or loss of the company for that period. In preparing those accounts the directors are required to:

- select suitable accounting policies and then apply them consistently;
- make judgements and estimates that are reasonable and prudent;
- prepare the accounts on a going concern basis unless it is inappropriate to presume that the company will continue in business.

The directors are responsible for keeping proper accounting records which disclose with reasonable accuracy at any time the financial position of the company and to enable them to ensure that the financial statements comply with the Companies Act. They are also responsible for safeguarding the assets of the company and hence for taking reasonable steps for the prevention and detection of fraud and other irregularities.

Principal activity

The principal activity of the company throughout the year was the sale and maintenance of office machinery.

Directors

The directors in office throughout the year were as follows:

A.B. Copier
C.D. Writer

On behalf of the board

C.D. Writer
Secretary
Date:

Appendix C.2 Small company statutory Profit and Loss Account format 1

A Small Company

Profit and Loss Account (Format 1)

For the Year Ended 30 September

	Notes	This Year £	Last Year £
Turnover		811,337	678,806
Cost of sales		583,229	495,214
Gross profit		228,108	183,592
Distribution costs		(77,943)	(65,524)
Administrative expenses		(90,723)	(83,430)
Operating profit	2	59,442	34,638
Profit on disposal of fixed assets		500	-
Interest receivable		230	-
Interest payable		(1,753)	(4,888)
Profit on ordinary activities before taxation		58,419	29,750
Taxation		(7,500)	(5,000)
Profit for the financial year	8	50,919	24,750

Appendix C.3 Small company Balance Sheet format 1

A Small Company

Balance Sheet as at 30 September

	Notes	This Year		Last Year	
		£	£	£	£
Tangible fixed assets	3		36,390		34,113
Current assets					
Stock		128,705		115,830	
Debtors	4	106,846		78,104	
Cash at bank and in hand		8,179		200	
		243,730		194,134	
Creditors: amounts falling due within one year	5	113,432		99,878	
Net current assets			130,298		94,256
Total assets less current liabilities			166,688		128,369
Creditors: amounts falling due after more than one year	6		(5,209)		(7,809)
Net assets			161,479		120,560
Capital and reserves					
Called up share capital	7		10,000		10,000
Profit and loss account	8		151,479		110,560
Shareholders' funds			161,479		120,560

Signed on behalf of the board of directors

....

A.B. Copier
Director

Appendix C.4 Small company Notes to the Accounts

<u>A Small Company</u>

<u>Notes to the Accounts</u>

<u>30 September</u>

1. Accounting policies

Basis of accounting

The accounts have been prepared under the historical cost convention and in accordance with the Financial Reporting Standard for Smaller Entities.

Turnover

Turnover represents the value, excluding Value Added Tax (VAT), of goods and services supplied to customers during the year.

Depreciation

Depreciation is provided to write off the cost of tangible fixed assets over their expected useful lives at the following rates:

Plant and machinery   –   15% straight line

Motor vehicles   –   25% straight line

Stock

Stock is valued at the lower of cost and net realisable value.

Leasing

Rentals payable under operating leases are charged to the Profit and Loss Account on a straight line basis over the period of the lease.

Tangible fixed assets acquired under finance leases or hire purchase are capitalised and depreciated in the same manner as other tangible fixed assets. The related obligations, net of future finance charges, are included in creditors. The interest element is charged to the Profit and Loss Account over the period of the lease at a constant proportion of the outstanding balance of capital repayments.

Appendix C.4 Small company Notes to the Accounts (continued)

2. Operating profit

Operating profit is stated after charging:

	This Year £	Last Year £
Directors' remuneration	70,000	60,000
Depreciation	12,203	11,470

3. Tangible fixed assets

	Total £	Plant & Machinery £	Motor Vehicles £
Cost			
At beginning of year	66,050	33,050	33,000
Additions	16,480	2,480	14,000
Disposals	(8,000)	-	(8,000)
At end of year	74,530	35,530	39,000
Depreciation			
At beginning of year	31,937	16,750	15,187
Provided for the year	12,203	3,828	8,375
On disposals	(6,000)	-	(6,000)
At end of year	38,140	20,578	17,562
Net book value			
At end of year	36,390	14,952	21,438
At end of last year	34,113	16,300	17,813

The net book value of motor vehicles includes £6,000 (last year £9,000) in respect of assets held under finance leases. Depreciation in respect of these assets amounted to £3,000 for the year (last year £3,000).

4. Debtors

	This Year £	Last Year £
Trade debtors	105,474	76,856
Prepayments	1,372	1,248
	106,846	78,104

5. Creditors: amounts falling due within one year

	This Year £	Last Year £
Bank overdraft	-	5,782
Obligations under finance leases	2,600	3,086
Trade creditors	86,147	73,051
Other creditors	1,929	815
Corporation Tax	7,500	5,000
Taxation and social security	12,446	10,519
Accruals	2,810	1,625
	113,432	99,878

6. Creditors: amounts due after more than one year

	This Year £	Last Year £
Obligations under finance leases	5,209	7,809

7. Share capital

	This Year £	Last Year £
Authorised		
50,000 ordinary shares of £1 each	50,000	50,000

Appendix C.4 Small company Notes to the Accounts (continued)

Allotted, called up and fully paid

10,000 ordinary shares of £1 each	10,000	10,000

8. Reserves

	Profit and Loss Account £
At beginning of year	110,560
Profit for the year	50,919
Ordinary dividends paid	(10,000)
At end of year	151,479

Appendix C.5 Small company detailed Profit and Loss Account

A Small Company

Detailed Trading and Profit and Loss Account

For the Year Ended 30 September

	This Year		Last Year	
	£	£	£	£
Sales				
Equipment	703,412		583,832	
Repairs	107,925		94,974	
		811,337		678,806
Cost of sales				
Opening stock	115,830		121,685	
Purchases	543,558		441,017	
Wages	52,546		48,342	
	711,934		611,044	
Closing stock	(128,705)		(115,830)	
		583,229		495,214
Gross profit		228,108		183,592
Other income				
Bank interest received		230		-
		228,338		183,592
Less: Expenses				
Establishment	20,858		21,192	
Selling and distribution	77,443		65,524	
Administration	66,558		58,634	
Financial	5,060		8,492	
		169,919		153,842
Net profit for the year		58,419		29,750

Appendix C.5 Small company detailed Profit and Loss Account (continued)

A Small Company

Details of Expenses

For the Year Ended 30 September

	This Year £	Last Year £
Establishment		
Rent and rates	13,500	13,260
Heat and light	2,728	2,183
Repairs and renewals	4,630	5,749
	20,858	21,192
Selling and distribution		
Director's remuneration	35,000	30,000
Salaries	18,400	16,250
Advertising	3,486	2,526
Motor and travelling	12,682	8,498
Depreciation – motor vehicles	8,375	8,250
Profit on vehicle disposal	(500)	–
	77,443	65,524
Administration		
Director's remuneration	35,000	30,000
Salaries	18,082	16,560
Printing and stationery	2,048	1,928
Telephone	2,227	1,995
Insurance	1,704	1,608
Accountancy	1,850	1,750
Legal and professional	1,235	1,175
Sundries	584	398
Depreciation – plant and machinery	3,828	3,220
	66,558	58,634
Financial		
Bad debts	2,787	2,984
Bank charges	520	620
Bank interest	1,009	4,060
Hire purchase interest	744	828
	5,060	8,492

Appendix D Small company Profit and Loss Account format 2

A Small Company

Profit and Loss Account (Format 2)

For the Year Ended 30 September

	Notes	This Year £	Last Year £
Turnover		811,337	678,806
Change in stocks of finished goods		12,875	(5,855)
Goods for resale		(543,558)	(441,017)
Staff costs		(159,028)	(141,152)
Depreciation on fixed assets		(12,203)	(11,470)
Other operating charges		(49,981)	(44,674)
Operating profit		59,442	34,638
Profit on disposal of fixed assets		500	-
Interest receivable		230	-
Interest payable		(1,753)	(4,888)
Profit on ordinary activities before taxation		58,419	29,750
Taxation		(7,500)	(5,000)
Profit for the financial year		50,919	24,750

Appendix E Medium company Cash Flow Statement

A Medium Company

Cash Flow Statement

For the Year Ended 30 September

	This Year		Last Year	
	£	£	£	£
Reconciliation of operating profit to net cash inflow from operating activities				
Operating profit		59,442		34,638
Depreciation		12,203		11,470
Increase in stocks		(12,875)		(14,638)
Increase in debtors		(28,742)		(16,725)
Increase in trade creditors		13,096		1,363
Increase/(decrease) in other creditors		4,226		(2,615)
Net cash inflow from operating activities		47,350		13,493
Returns on investments and servicing of finance				
Interest received	230		-	
Interest paid	(1,753)		(4,888)	
Dividends paid	(10,000)		-	
		(11,523)		(4,888)
Taxation		(5,000)		(2,200)
Capital expenditure				
Payments to acquire tangible fixed assets	(16,480)		(11,500)	
Receipts from sales of tangible fixed assets	2,500		-	
		(13,980)		(11,500)
		16,847		(5,095)

Appendix E Medium company Cash Flow Statement (continued)

Financing

Capital element of hire purchase repayments	(3,086)	(3,400)
Increase/(decrease) in cash	13,761	(8,495)
Net (debt)/funds at start of year	(5,582)	2,913
Net funds/(debt) at end of year	8,179	(5,582)

Appendix F Small company Cash Flow Statement

A Small Company

Cash Flow Statement

For the Year Ended 30 September

	This Year		Last Year	
	£	£	£	£
Cash generated from operations				
Operating profit		59,442		34,638
Depreciation		12,203		11,470
Increase in stocks		(12,875)		(14,638)
Increase in debtors		(28,742)		(16,725)
Increase in trade creditors		13,096		1,363
Increase/(decrease) in other creditors		4,226		(2,615)
Cash generated from operations		47,350		13,493
Cash from other sources				
Interest received	230			
Proceeds from sale of fixed assets	2,500		-	
		2,730		-
		50,080		13,493
Application of cash				
Interest paid	1,753		4,888	
Tax paid	5,000		2,200	
Dividends paid	10,000		-	
Purchase of fixed assets	16,480		11,500	
Hire purchase repayments	3,086		3,400	
		36,319		21,988

Appendix F Small company Cash Flow Statement (continued)

Net increase/ (decrease) in cash	13,761	(8,495)
Cash at bank and in hand less overdraft at start of year	(5,582)	2,913
Cash at bank and in hand less overdraft at end of year	8,179	(5,582)
Consisting of:		
Cash at bank and in hand	8,179	200
Overdraft	-	(5,782)
	8,179	(5,582)

Appendix G.1 Receipts and Payments Account (vertical)

A Club

Receipts and Payments Account (Vertical)

For the Year Ended 30 June

	£
Receipts	
Members' subscriptions	2,800
Fundraising activities	723
Sale of badges	64
Sale of equipment	150
Bank interest	12
Total receipts	3,749
Payments	
Purchase of badges	50
Hire of room	250
Purchase of equipment	1,230
Repairs to equipment	178
Travelling expenses	643
Insurance	225
Printing and stationery	319
	2,895
Net receipts	854
Cash at bank and in hand	
At beginning of year	326
At end of year	1,180

Appendix G.2 Receipts and Payments Account (horizontal)

A Club

Receipts and Payments Account (Horizontal)

For the Year Ended 30 June

Receipts	£	Payments	£
Cash at bank and in hand at beginning of year	326	Purchase of badges	50
Members' subscriptions	2,800	Hire of room	250
Fundraising activities	723	Purchase of equipment	1,230
Sale of badges	64	Repairs to equipment	178
Sale of equipment	150	Travelling expenses	643
Bank interest	12	Insurance	225
		Printing and stationery	319
		Cash at bank and in hand at end of year	1,180
Total	4,075	Total	4,075

Appendix H Checklist for reviewing accounts

Trading and Profit and Loss Account

1. Review sales and compare them with the previous period.
   Consider whether the increases/decreases are due to price
   or volume changes. ❏

2. Compare sales with budgets. ❏

3. Confirm that the sales figure is the same as that declared on
   the VAT returns for the period, or obtain reasons for the
   differences. ❏

4. Where each item sold is easily identified reconcile the sales
   figure with the number of items sold. ❏

5. If sales are on a contract basis (e.g. construction or
   engineering), agree the sales figure with the sum of the
   individual contracts. ❏

6. If there are branches, confirm that sales for all branches have
   been included. ❏

7. If figures are available for the industry generally, compare
   the sales figures with the industry trends. ❏

8. Review the gross profit percentage and compare it with the
   previous period and budgets.
   Gross profit/sales x 100 (expressed as a percentage)
   Consider the reasons for changes. ❏

9. Compare the gross profit percentage with figures available
   for the industry. ❏

10. Review expenses and compare them with the previous period
    and budgets.
    Consider the reasons for changes. ❏

11. Calculate the average wage cost per employee and compare
    it with the previous year. ❏

12. Confirm that expenses, such as rent, rates, electricity, etc.,
    cover the full period and no more. ❏

13. Review items that might be expected to change in relation to
    each other (e.g. sales commissions in relation to sales). ❏

Appendix H Checklist for reviewing accounts (continued)

14. Confirm that any private expenses and private proportions have been dealt with correctly (e.g. motor expenses, telephone, etc.). ❏

15. Calculate any relevant sales statistics and compare them with the previous period and budgets (e.g. commission as a percentage of sales, delivery charges as a percentage of sales, sales per square metre, sales per salesperson). ❏

16. Confirm that no fixed asset additions have been incorrectly shown as expenses in the Profit and Loss Account. ❏

17. Obtain an analysis of sundry expenses, if significant. ❏

18. In a company, consider whether dividends should be paid. ❏

19. In a company, consider whether the tax charge appears reasonable in relation to the net profit. The tax charge in the Profit and Loss Account might be expected to equate to the rate of Corporation Tax payable, but there can be good reasons why this is not the case. ❏

   If there is a tax loss, ascertain whether the losses are available to set off against past or future taxable profits. Consult your accountant on tax matters. Information is also available on www.hmrc.gov.uk. ❏

20. If the accounts are for a sole trader or partnership, ascertain details of any tax payable or recoverable. Your accountant will advise. ❏

Balance Sheet

21. Review movements in fixed assets for additions and disposals. ❏
   Confirm that all known additions and disposals have been included and that there are no items included in additions that should have been written off to the Profit and Loss Account. ❏

22. Confirm that the correct rate of depreciation has been charged against the fixed assets. ❏

23. Consider whether any further depreciation should be provided. ❏

Appendix H Checklist for reviewing accounts (continued)

24. Consider whether property should be revalued. ❑

25. Consider whether any items included in fixed assets are
    no longer used in the business and should be written off. ❑

26. Consider whether the Balance Sheet totals are positive
    (total net assets) or negative (total net liabilities). ❑

27. Consider whether there are net current assets or liabilities. ❑

28. Calculate the current ratio and compare it with the
    previous period.
    Current assets/current liabilities ❑

29. Calculate the quick (or acid test) ratio and compare it with
    the previous period.
    Current assets less stock/current liabilities ❑

30. Review stock and work-in-progress and compare them
    with the previous period.
    Calculate the average stockholding period and compare it
    with the previous period.
    Stock/cost of stock purchased per day ❑

31. Review debtors and compare them with the previous period.
    Calculate the average collection period (debtor days) and
    compare it with the previous period.
    Debtors/credit sales per day ❑

32. Review creditors and compare them with the previous period.
    Calculate the average payment period (creditor days) and
    compare it with the previous period.
    Creditors/credit purchases per day ❑

33. Review the proprietors' funds (for a company, share capital and
    reserves; for a sole trader or partnership, capital and current
    accounts) and account for movements from the previous period. ❑

34. Sole trader or partnership – review the details of cash
    introduced into the business. ❑

35. Sole trader or partnership – review details of the drawings. ❑

Appendix H Checklist for reviewing accounts (continued)

36. Review all other Balance Sheet items and compare them
with the previous period.   ❏

**Other ratios: compare with the previous period and available
industry statistics**

37. Return on capital employed
Profit before interest and taxation/capital employed   ❏

38. Interest cover
Profit before interest/interest   ❏

39. Earnings per share
Profit after tax/number of issued shares   ❏

40. Dividends per share
Dividends payable/number of issued shares   ❏

41. Dividend cover
Profit after tax/dividends   ❏

42. Yield
*Dividend per share/amount paid per share x 100
(expressed as a percentage)*   ❏

43. Price/earnings ratio
Price paid per share/earnings per share   ❏

44. Balance Sheet gearing
*Borrowings/shareholders' funds x 100
(expressed as a percentage)*   ❏

Other matters

45. Review Notes to the Accounts and confirm that any
exceptional items have been fully explained.   ❏

46. Confirm that information concerning transactions with
related parties has been fully disclosed.   ❏

47. Confirm that the business is a going concern.   ❏

48. Consider whether any other figures require further
explanation.   ❏

Appendix I Troubleshooting checklist

Checklist showing some of the warning signs that may indicate a business heading for trouble.

1. Customers are taking longer to pay. ❏

2. Major customers are in financial difficulty. ❏

3. You are delaying payments to suppliers and other creditors. ❏

4. Management accounts show that the business is making losses. ❏

5. The actual results and/or cash flow performance are worse than the forecast. ❏

6. Sales are declining. ❏

7. Profit margins are declining. ❏

8. Overhead expenses show significant increases without corresponding increases in sales. ❏

9. The bank balance is constantly up to the agreed overdraft limit. ❏

10. Stock levels are excessive for the amount of business being carried out. ❏

11. There are significant amounts of obsolete stocks. ❏

12. There is a lack of orders for future work. ❏

13. Old fixed assets (plant and machinery, etc.) are not being replaced because funds are not available. ❏

14. Maintenance work is not being carried out on property and other fixed assets because funds are not available. ❏

15. There is an unsatisfactory relationship with the employees. ❏

16. There is significant dependence on one customer. ❏

17. There is significant dependence on one supplier. ❏

18. There is significant dependence on key staff who may be unsettled or in ill-health. ❏

19. The business operates from leased premises with only a short time before the lease expires. ❏

Appendix I Troubleshooting checklist (continued)

20. Machinery is obsolete. ❏

21. There are significant new technical developments in the industry, which require investment and training. ❏

22. Competitors are introducing new products. ❏

23. There are new competitors in the market. ❏

24. There are legal proceedings against the business. ❏

25. Other businesses in the same industry are failing. ❏

26. There is new government legislation that will affect the operation of the business. ❏

27. A key franchise or patent is lost by the business. ❏

Checklist of action that may be considered when problems have been identified.

1. Get professional advice at an early stage:
   - Accountant ❏
   - Banker ❏
   - Solicitor ❏
   - Surveyor ❏
   - Trade association ❏
   - Insolvency practitioner ❏

2. Take note and act on management information:
   - Management accounts and budgets ❏
   - Cash Flow Statement and forecast ❏
   - Aged list of debtors ❏
   - Aged list of creditors ❏

3. Monitor bank balances daily. ❏

4. Ensure that invoices are sent to customers as soon as a sale is made. ❏

5. Send statements to customers promptly at the end of each month. ❏

Appendix I Troubleshooting checklist (continued)

6. Follow up slow payers:
    - Telephone calls ❏
    - Visits ❏
    - Letters ❏
    - Place in debt collector's hands ❏

7. Stop future sales to customers until outstanding
    debts are cleared. ❏

8. Consider offering discounts for early payment. ❏

9. Consider charging customers interest for late payment. ❏

10. Discuss extended credit terms with your suppliers. ❏

11. Look for new suppliers offering better terms than your
    existing suppliers. ❏

12. Consider ways to increase sales figures:
    - Increase prices ❏
    - Reduce prices to increase the volume of sales ❏
    - Advertising ❏
    - Look for other markets, including exports ❏
    - Increase production ❏
    - Extend range of products sold ❏
    - Sell slow moving stocks at reduced prices ❏

13. Reduce purchases or production until excess stocks are sold. ❏

14. Consider operating the business on a smaller scale. ❏

15. Consider reducing staff levels. ❏

16. Consider employing part-time staff or using sub-contract
    labour instead of full-time employees. ❏

17. Put additional finance into the business:
    - Personal loan ❏
    - Issue additional shares ❏
    - Increase bank overdraft facilities ❏
    - Bank loan ❏

Appendix I Troubleshooting checklist (continued)

    - Loans from relatives or friends ❑

    - Debt factoring (Debt factoring involves the business transferring the debts owing by its customers to a finance organisation ('the factor') and obtaining loans secured on the debts. Further information can be found at www. businesslink.gov.uk.) ❑

    - Purchase fixed assets on hire purchase instead of cash ❑

    - Lease fixed assets instead of purchasing ❑

    - Sell fixed assets that are not required in the business ❑

    - Apply for grants ❑

    - Rent out surplus property ❑

18. Obtain key man insurance for key staff. This type of insurance will make a payment to the business in the event of the death or disability of a key member of staff. ❑

19. If the lease on the business premises is due to expire in the near future, negotiate a new lease at an early stage or look for new premises in advance of the expiration of the existing lease. ❑

20. Train staff to use new techniques. ❑

21. Develop new products. ❑

22. Do not delay payment of VAT, or other taxes, as severe penalties could be imposed on the business. If necessary, discuss the position with your accountant, bank manager and government department. ❑

23. Do not send out cheques that you know are likely to bounce. If necessary, discuss the position with your accountant, bank manager and suppliers. ❑

24. Do not continue trading if you know that the business cannot pay its debts as they fall due. A company director may be held personally liable if a company continues to trade in these circumstances. ❑

Appendix J Stocktaking and stock valuation checklist

Stocktaking procedures

1. Stocktaking instructions should provide for the following:
   - All locations are covered by the count. ❏
   - Slow moving, obsolete and damaged stock will be identified on the stock sheets. ❏
   - Any stock belonging to third parties is identified and properly dealt with. ❏
   - Stocks are counted methodically to ensure that all items are counted and no items are included in the count more than once. ❏
   - Sufficient details are included in the stock sheets to make it easy for items to be identified at a later date. ❏
   - The issue and return of stock sheets is controlled. ❏
   - Any stock movements during the count are recorded so that appropriate adjustments can be made. ❏

2. Stock sheets should show at least the following for each stock line:
   - Product reference number, if relevant. ❏
   - Description of stock. ❏
   - Quantity counted. ❏
   - Value of each item. ❏
   - Total value (*quantity counted x value of each item*). ❏

3. Stock sheets should be numbered consecutively before being used so that they can all be accounted for after the stocktake. ❏

4. The stocktake can be carried out more quickly if descriptions of all the stock lines held are written on the stock sheets before the count starts. It is then only necessary to write in the quantities as they are counted. You will also need some blank sheets in case any stock items are found in addition to those for which descriptions are shown. ❏

5. If stock records are kept showing quantities held, these quantities should not be entered on the stock sheets in advance of the stocktake. ❏

6. Counting will be made easier if all stores areas are kept tidy. ❏

Appendix J Stocktaking and stock valuation checklist (continued)

7. It is usually best to start counting at one end of the store and continue in a methodical manner to the other end. This will help to ensure that all items are counted and no items are included in the count more than once. ❏

8. A mark or label put on the stock items or shelves after each item has been counted will help to make sure that nothing is counted more than once. ❏

9. If possible, carry out the stocktake in pairs, with one person counting while the other records the quantities on the stock sheets. ❏

10. If any queries arise during the stocktake, they should be dealt with immediately. There may be subsequent stock movements making it difficult for you to clear up queries at a later stage. ❏

11. During the count, identify slow moving, obsolete and damaged stock and make a note of the details on the stock sheets. This is important as it may be necessary to reduce the value of these items when the figures are finalised. ❏

12. Make sure that any stock belonging to third parties (e.g. customers' stock awaiting repairs) is not included with your own stock details. ❏

13. Details of stock written on the stock sheets should be clear enough for all items to be identified at a later stage. ❏

14. Make a note of any stock movements during the count so that appropriate adjustments can be made. For example:

    - An item counted and recorded on the stock sheets could subsequently be sold to a customer before the close of business. Without an adjustment, the item could be included in both stock and sales with the result that profits are overstated in the accounts. The appropriate treatment would normally be to omit the item from the final stock figure and include it in the sales. ❏

    - A delivery into the store on the last day of the financial year should normally be included in the accounts as a purchase for the year and entered on the stock sheets. If the delivery takes place after the stock has been counted (but before the end of the day), it could be omitted from the stock sheets but included in the purchases. The result would be an understatement of

Appendix J Stocktaking and stock valuation checklist (continued)

profits in the accounts. The appropriate treatment would normally be to include the item in the final stock figure as well as in the purchases (assuming it has not been sold before the end of the day and included in the sales). ❏

15. Make a note of the last item delivered into stock before the stocktake begins. This can be followed up later to make sure that the item is included in both the stock and purchases figures. ❏

16. Make a note of the last item despatched to a customer before the stocktake begins. This can be followed up later to make sure that the item is included in the sales but not in the stock figures. ❏

17. Transfers of stock between different locations should be carefully recorded to make sure that the same stock is not included in the count at more than one location or omitted entirely. ❏

18. In some circumstances (e.g. where the same stock lines are kept in a number of different areas), it may be convenient to record the count on rough stock sheets before bringing the figures together on the final stock sheets. Transfers of figures from one sheet to another should be checked carefully to make sure that nothing is omitted or included more than once. ❏

19. If stock records are kept, at the end of the stocktake, compare the quantities counted with the stock records. Investigate any significant differences immediately and amend stock records or stock sheets as necessary. ❏

Stock valuation

When all the stock has been counted it needs to be evaluated.

1. Stock is normally valued at the lower of cost or net realisable value. ❏

2. Net realisable value is the estimated selling price after taking into account any further completion costs and selling, marketing and distribution costs. ❏

3. As a general rule, profit is not included in the accounts until stock is sold. ❏

4. In some circumstances, where there is long-term contract work-in-progress, it may be appropriate to include some profit in the

Appendix J Stocktaking and stock valuation checklist (continued)

accounts before the contract has been completed. Your accountant will advise you. ❏

5. Where the business does not involve manufacturing, the stock price is normally the purchase price, less any trade discounts, shown on the supplier's invoice. If parts of any stock line were bought at significantly different prices, it may be necessary to look at more than one invoice. Otherwise, the whole of the stock line can be valued at the price shown on the last purchase invoice before the year end. ❏

6. Where items in stock have been purchased at prices shown on suppliers' price lists, it may save time to use the price lists for stock pricing instead of referring to invoices. Any trade discounts should be taken into account. ❏

7. Where the business involves manufacturing or provides a service, the cost of stock and work-in-progress normally includes labour, as well as materials. The way in which labour costs are calculated will depend on the type of business and the records kept, but they should represent the cost of the employees' time in carrying out the manufacturing process or providing the service. If in doubt, consult your accountant. ❏

8. Where products are manufactured by the business, a standard cost, including materials and labour, may have been established for each product. Standard costs should be reviewed regularly to take account of changes in suppliers' prices and wages costs, as well as any changes in the manufacturing process. ❏

9. Where standard costs are not used, the labour part of stock and work-in-progress may be calculated by reference to time sheets and rates of pay. In some cases, a system of work-in-progress records may provide the information. ❏

10. It may be appropriate to include overheads as part of the cost of some stock and work-in-progress, in addition to materials and labour. Discuss this with your accountant. ❏

11. In some cases the most convenient way to value stock is to start with the selling price and deduct the profit to arrive at the

Appendix J Stocktaking and stock valuation checklist (continued)

cost. This method will only produce accurate results if the profit margins are consistent and it is not generally recommended. ❏

12. Stock should only be given a value if it is expected to be sold. Old, obsolete and damaged stock may only be saleable at less than normal prices and this should be taken into account. ❏

13. Before spending time on the stock valuation, agree the method of valuation with your accountant.

❏

Appendix K The treatment of Value Added Tax (VAT) in the accounts

Outline

VAT is added to the selling price of goods or services by businesses registered for VAT. The tax must then be paid to the Customs arm of HM Revenue & Customs (HMRC). The tax on sales is called 'output tax'.

For example, if a business is selling a product for £100 before adding VAT, the standard VAT rate of 17.5 per cent is added to make the total selling price £117.50. The VAT amount of £17.50 must be paid to HMRC and this is recovered from the customer when he pays for the goods.

When the business buys goods and services from other suppliers, VAT will be included in the purchase price if the supplier is also VAT registered. The tax on purchases is called 'input tax'.

For example, if a business buys goods or services costing £100 before VAT has been added, the standard VAT rate of 17.5 per cent is added by the supplier to make the total purchase price £117.50. The VAT-registered business buying those goods or services can reclaim the input VAT of £17.50 from HMRC.

In practice, the business will deduct input tax from output tax and pay the balance to HMRC. If input tax is more than output tax, the excess will be paid to the business by HMRC.

Broadly, apart from the costs of administration, there is no cost to a business registered for VAT as the output tax is collected from customers and the input tax that has been paid to suppliers is recovered from HMRC.

A business that is not registered for VAT does not add VAT to the selling price of its goods and does not have to pay any VAT to HMRC. However, it will still have to pay input tax on goods and services supplied by VAT-registered suppliers and it is unable to recover this tax from HMRC. In the accounts, this input tax is included with the expense item and is not shown separately.

Example

The example on the following page illustrates how VAT is treated in the accounts of a business registered for VAT. The transactions shown are for a period of three months to 31 March.

Appendix K The treatment of Value Added Tax (VAT) in the accounts (continued)

Transactions with customers

	Sales Before VAT £	VAT @ 17.5% £	Total Sales Price £
Invoiced to customers	100,000	17,500	117,500
Cash received from customers	80,000	14,000	94,000
Owing by customers at 31 March	20,000	3,500	23,500

Transactions with suppliers for goods and services

	Purchases Before VAT £	VAT @ 17.5% £	Total Purchases Price £
Invoiced by suppliers	60,000	10,500	70,500
Paid to suppliers	30,000	5,250	35,250
Owing to suppliers at 31 March	30,000	5,250	35,250

VAT account

	£
Output tax on sales	17,500
Input tax on purchases and expenses	10,500
Amount owing to HMRC at 31 March	7,000

Bank account

	£
Received from customers	94,000
Paid to suppliers	35,250
Balance at bank at 31 March	58,750

Appendix K The treatment of Value Added Tax (VAT) in the accounts (continued)

Profit and Loss Account for the three months to 31 March

	£
Sales	100,000
Purchases and expenses	60,000
Net profit	40,000

Balance Sheet at 31 March

	£	£
Current assets		
Owing by customers	23,500	
Bank account	58,750	
		82,250
Creditors		
Suppliers	35,250	
Customs	7,000	
		42,250
Net assets		40,000
Profit retained in the business		40,000

Index